New Testament Ministries

Meat of the Word

Book Three

New convert care program

A Scriptural follow-up program that works

Dr. James Wilkins

"… grow in GRACE, and *in* the KNOWLEDGE of our Lord and Saviour Jesus Christ …"
II PETER 3:18

Meat of the Word is the third book in the new convert care and development series.

Printed By:

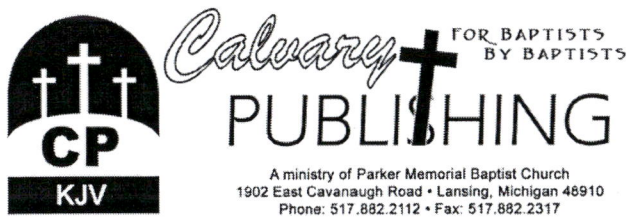

FOR BAPTISTS
BY BAPTISTS

Calvary PUBLISHING

CP KJV

A ministry of Parker Memorial Baptist Church
1902 East Cavanaugh Road • Lansing, Michigan 48910
Phone: 517.882.2112 • Fax: 517.882.2317

www.calvarypublishing.org

TABLE OF CONTENTS

SIMPLE STEPS IN USING THIS BOOK

1. Complete the first book in this series, Milk of the Word

2. We suggest that the same Big Brother continue meeting with the student.

3. The Role Model introduces the book to him. He goes over the *"Dear Disciple"* letter and fills in the blanks on the Prayer List Page.

4. The Role Model reads Faith Builder Page and explains how to do it each morning and evening.

5. The Big Brother explains the grading procedure; that the new member is to read all of the lessons through before answering the questions.

6. The student fills in the blanks on the day designated, Monday's on Monday - Tuesday's on Tuesday, etc. Review the previous day's answers before doing the current exercise for better retention of material.

7. The Role Model assigns the proper grade.

A = excellent: did his work on daily basis
B = good: did all the work but not on a daily basis
J – Future Judgment – Did not complete the work

8. The Role Model has prayer, leaves and makes his report.

MY PRAYER LIST

MATTHEW 6:6 "...enter into thy closet,... shut thy door..." This statement indicates that believers are to pray audibly. Address God in a reverent way and pray for definite requests.

DEAR HEAVENLY FATHER ....

1. **I'LL PRAY FOR MYSELF** - for a humble, submissive spirit to Christ for forgiveness.
2. **FOR MY FAMILY** - that I may be a Christian testimony and blessing to each one of them.
3. **FOR MY PASTOR** - that God will give him the grace, spiritual power and wisdom to lead, feed and shepherd the flock.
4. **FOR MY COUNTRY** - that God will send revival, especially to those in high positions.
5. **FOR YOUR MISSIONARIES** - for their safety, success and support. (Write down missionaries' names and their countries)
1. _____ country _____
2. _____ country _____
3. _____ country _____
6. FOR **MY LOST LOVED ONES AND FRIENDS** - Write down at least three people who you will pray for daily.
1. _____ Date Prayer Answered_____
2. _____ Date Prayer Answered_____
3. _____ Date Prayer Answered_____

7. **FOR EVANGELISTS AND OTHER SPECIAL WORKERS** - Call them by Name.
    1. Evangelist James Wilkins

In Jesus Name, Amen

DEAR DISCIPLE,

Paul commanded the believers in Hebrews 6:1 to **"…go on unto perfection..."** [*spiritual maturity*]. Meat of the Word is presented to enable the new convert to develop this spiritual maturity and have stronger convictions which will DIRECT HIS LIFE!

Far too many believers live off *"the pastor's"* convictions, or *"mom and dad's"* convictions.

Other believers do not have convictions but are directed by "*preferences*" which change as the situation changes.

These lessons are presented to help you establish your own convictions and give you a clearer understanding of your life's purpose in the light of eternity.

In order for the student to obtain the MOST OUT of this book he must DO TWO THINGS.

FIRST, HE MUST FOLLOW THE METHOD which enables people to retain the most information. Zig Zigler, the noted Christian motivator states, **"The average person who reads something once retains only 6% of what he reads two weeks later"**. **But the person who reads the material once each day for 6 consecutive days will retain 62% of what he read**. So, for best results the student is admonished to review the previous day's activity before performing the exercise for the current day.

Go over the FAITH BUILDER and review the DAILY QUESTIONS each day.

SECONDLY, HE MUST UNDERSTAND HOW THE DEVIL ATTACKS and fortify himself against the devil's attacks. The devil will attack the believer through the mind. Memorize the Daily Declarations and Scripture verses in order to use them as a shield of faith against the fiery darts (thoughts) which the devil will shoot into one's mind. Believe the Bible instead of one's doubts or thoughts.

In studying these lessons one will obtain a greater awareness of his purpose in the light of eternal things which will develop strong personal convictions.

If one will study these lessons and follow the method outlined, the author will guarantee your spiritual growth. This spiritual growth will lead to stronger personal convictions, success and happiness.

May God help you to become a champion for Christ. (John 10:10)

Yours for Christ's Glory
James Wilkins

FOR ADDED BLESSING AND GROWTH

"For as he thinketh in his heart, so *is* he ..."
PROV. 23:7

This verse presents one of the greatest principles in the BIBLE. This statement declares the fact — what a person thinks is what he is.

- If one takes into HIS mind negative, worldly thoughts then he will LIVE A WORLDLY and a negative life.
- If he takes into his mind positive and spiritual thoughts then he will live a happy life of faith.
- One can change a poor self-image by developing good, positive habits.
- One can transform himself and increase his faith by doing three things:
  1. MAJOR ON GOOD, HEALTHY THOUGHTS
  2. STATE HIS POSITIVE GOALS REGULARLY
  3. WASH HIS MIND BY READING AND MEMORIZING THE SCRIPTURES
- One can develop a good, happy inner self by this simple DAILY EXERCISE:

  A MUST - State the FAITH BUILDING principles - morning and evening

  A MUST - Strive to memorize the verse each week.

DAILY FAITH BUILDER

LESSON ONE

GOD'S CONCERN FOR HIS CHILDREN

Special Thought for the Week

The Lord loves me so much that in His most agonizing hour His thoughts were of me.

Daily Declaration

God has designed my life to be lived in the light of eternity and promises never to leave or forsake me.

CHECK BLOCK AFTER REPEATING

	Mon	Tues	Wed	Thurs	Fri	Sat	Sun
A.M.							
P.M							

Memory Verse

"For our light affliction, which is but for a moment, worketh for us a far more exceeding *and* eternal weight of glory;" II CORINTHIANS 4:17

Special Goal to Obtain

I will strive to help someone with *"THEIR PROBLEM"* this week.

LESSON ONE

GOD'S CONCERN FOR HIS CHILDREN

INTRODUCTION: In **HEBREWS 12:5**, Paul said that God, **"...speaketh unto you as unto children..."(+)** This statement was never truer than in the words Jesus spoke in John 13:1, through John 16:13. These words of concern are followed by the wonderful prayer of Jesus for His disciples. John 17:1-26. In this setting, Jesus uses the expression, **"These things have I spoken unto you..."** five different times. Please study the whole context, but particularly note the love and concern which is revealed in the five verses which begin with that expression.

MONDAY
I. WORDS SPOKEN TO PREPARE
FOR HIS DEPARTURE

"These things have I spoken unto you, being *yet* present with you." JOHN 14:25

A.   A TENDER TIME

When He spoke these words, Jesus had finished his earthly ministry. Only His death on the cross remains. Three and one-half years had been spent training and developing His disciples. Now He must leave them. In John's Gospel, Chapters 13-17, one of the tenderest scenes in the Bible is recorded.

Jesus begins by saying, **"These things have I spoken unto you, being *yet* present with**

you." He is saying, *while I am yet alive I am telling you something to remember when I am gone.* His thoughts were for them. He was preparing them by reminding them that in His most trying hour He cared. He was unselfishly thinking of them and their welfare.

B.   A TRANSITIONAL TIME

The apostles were so accustomed to having Jesus with them, if there was a problem, Jesus would settle it. If there was a question, Jesus would answer it. If there was a need, Jesus would meet it—but that period ends now. After this night, things will never be the same again. The apostles must learn to live without hearing His voice.

From this night on they must remember His word. By faith, they must follow His teaching and trust the leading of the unseen Holy Spirit. **(+)** Jesus speaks tenderly to help them in this trying, transitional time.

C.   A TESTIMONIAL TIME

As Jesus manifests His love, His tenderness, and His concern for these disciples when they face one of their darkest hours, so does He manifest Himself to every one of His children in their time of difficulty. Paul speaks of the tender heart of Jesus and how He is touched with "**... the feeling of our infirmities ...**" in **HEBREWS 4:15. (+)**

Jesus knows and cares about the needs of every one of His children. **(+)** He "**... is a friend** *that* **sticketh closer than a brother.**" **PROVERBS**

18:24 (+) He **"... will never leave thee, nor forsake thee." HEBREWS 13:5**. He even goes with the believer where father or mother, friend or brother cannot—**"...through the valley of the shadow of death..." PSALM 23:4**. This tender-hearted Jesus is always mindful of your heartache. He sees your tears and can meet every individual need. Jesus knows and cares.

TUESDAY
II. WORDS SPOKEN TO STIMULATE
THE BELIEVER'S JOY

"These things have I spoken unto you, that my joy might remain in you, and *that* your joy might be full." JOHN 15:11 (+)

A.   THE JOY OF SINS FORGIVEN

Remember the joy you experienced when you knew that your sins were forgiven?

- The guilt was gone!
- The burden was lifted!
- The peace of God was so sweet!
- The love of God was so real!
- Everything was new and wonderful!

Remember when you were first saved? Many people say, *"Boy, I wish I was as happy in the Lord as I was then."* You can have that same joy.

B.   THE JOY MIGHT CONTINUE

The expression, **"...that my joy might remain..."** indicates that the believer can lose the joy of salvation. **(+)** In fact, one has only to look around in the average fundamental church to see that many of God's children seem to have lost the joy of God in their soul. If they have the joy of God in their hearts, then their hearts have forgotten to tell their faces about it. **(+)** The faces of the average Sunday morning attendee do not reflect joy. They arrive at church, put on their *"happy faces"* and then go on in.

Many people can look back longingly and remember the joy they experienced when they were first saved. But somewhere along the way they have lost that freshness, that wonder, that illuminating joy. Jesus spoke to His disciples so the joy of God might continue in them and even grow and become a full or complete joy.

C. THE JOY MIGHT BECOME FULL

Jesus came that the believer might have eternal life and have it more abundantly. **JOHN 10:10**. This declaration follows the statement, **"The thief cometh not, but for to steal, and to kill, and to destroy ..."** In a world of death, trouble, trials and destruction, Jesus came that the believer could be happy, victorious, joyous and overcoming. **(+)**

In the closing hour of his earthly ministry, Jesus comforts His disciples by reassuring them. He tells them once again that His will and desire for their life is that their joy may be full.

Jesus wants His children to be happy. **(+)** He has designed a process of spiritual growth so the believer who follows God's plan for his life will experience continual joy.

Unless a child is properly loved, instructed and developed when he is young, he will have a difficult time adjusting to and living a happy life as an adult. One severe jolt which the child experiences may alter his life forever. So it is with God's spiritual children. In that trying hour, Jesus worked with them to make the experience one that would strengthen instead of weakening them.

In these perilous days of uncertainties, world crisis and ungodliness we must learn to help strengthen God's children in His word and Grace so the believer's joy may be full.

WEDNESDAY
III. WORDS SPOKEN WHICH PROTECT FROM OFFENCES

"These things have I spoken unto you, that ye should not be offended." JOHN 16:1(+)

A.   FACT OF COMING OFFENCES

The new convert is so thrilled with his new life. The joy and happiness of being saved is so wonderful that he cannot even imagine that he will ever be hurt or offended. **(+)** Generally when offences do come he is completely unprepared for them. It knocks him completely down and he becomes wounded. That is the reason Jesus said, **"These things have I spoken unto you, that ye should not be offended."** He is trying to offset and cushion them from some of the problems and trials they will soon encounter in life.

B.   THE FORCE OF THESE OFFENCES

The question arises in the new convert's mind, *"Where will these offences come and why?"* What is the force or source of these offences?

Offences will come from the world system. "If the world hate you, ye know that it hated me before *it hated* you." JOHN 15:18

Offence comes because the believer's joy, assurance and Christian life bring conviction and awareness of sin to the sinner. Take your Bible and read John 15:21-25. DO NOT be offended at the coolness, criticism or rejection of your closest friend or loved one. **(+)** Their problem is not with you, it is with their own selves and God. Keep a good attitude and continue to love, pray for and work with them until they are saved. **(+)**

Offences from other religious groups. Read John' 6:2-3. Many of your friends and loved ones are controlled by fears or traditions which have dominated their lives and childhood. They cannot help striking back. You are a threat to their security and hope of heaven. If what you believe is right, then they are wrong. If they are wrong, then they are lost. That brings fear and uncertainty, so they strike back.

Offences will come from the Devil.
The devil as a constant enemy, continually seeks to tempt, ensnare and destroy God's children. I Peter 5:8, James 4:7.

C.   **REASON FOR THESE OFFENCES OR PROBLEMS**

Jesus wanted His disciples to be alerted to these offences so they could be ready for them. **(+)**

He wanted them to be constantly aware of their enemy, the devil.

He wanted them to know that many of their problems would result from their association with Him. When a child of God follows Jesus in the paths of righteousness and does the things which satisfy God and bring happiness to the believer it brings conviction to the lost, especially to the religious lost. This will bring a counter-attack from them which results in these offences.

THURSDAY
IV. WORDS SPOKEN AS A TENDER PARENT

"These things have I spoken unto you in proverbs: but the time cometh, when I shall no more speak unto you in proverbs, but I shall shew you plainly of the Father." JOHN 16:25

A.   **AS A TENDER PARENT**

Many times little children ask questions which, if answered, would completely overwhelm them. **(+)** A wise parent answers such questions in a way as to protect the child from the harmful effects. Jesus, in the role of a loving parent, tells His disciples, "I have deliberately talked to you in proverbs." Some of the things you have asked about, you do not have enough spiritual growth to understand at this time. If you were told plainly they would be a hindrance instead of a help. The time will come when you will be shown plainly.

B.   AS A PROTECTIVE PARENT

In verse 12, Jesus speaks more pointedly to the disciples on this subject. He said, **"I have yet many things to say unto you, but ye CANNOT BEAR them now." (+)** He is speaking to them as a protective parent. His desire is to develop them into strong, spirit-filled leaders who are able to stand pressure, face death, and still keep a sweet, loving disposition. In order to do this, they must be protected and allowed to grow naturally into maturity.

A baby needs to be fed, loved, and allowed to grow without heartbreak or pressure in order to become a mature, well-adjusted, happy adult. **(+)**

A new convert needs careful, loving leadership after he is saved. He needs to follow the same procedure spiritually as a natural baby receives physically. There are some things he does not need to know! If he knew them, it would only hurt or discourage him.

Young convert, when you begin to hear something negative about the church, the pastor or what someone did—DO NOT ask questions! Get away from that person and keep right on serving the Lord. Your curiosity may be harmful to you. **(+)**

In times of uncertainty do what Paul commanded in **HEBREWS 13:7, "Remember them which have the rule over you,** [God placed them over you] **who have spoken unto you the word of God: whose faith follow..." (+)** In verse 17, Paul speaks even more strongly. It is vital that the new convert be protected and sheltered. He said, **"Obey them that have the rule over you, and submit yourselves: for they watch for your souls, as they that must give account, that they may do it with joy, and not with grief: for that** *is* **unprofitable FOR YOU."** Submit yourself to your pastor. You do not need to know as much as he knows—trust him and follow his faith.

C.   AS AN ASSURING PARENT

Remember, I Love you. John 13:34-15:9. This knowledge gives the believer real comfort.

God, the Father, loves you. John 14:23-24. This should give the believer double comfort.

Jesus prayed for the protection and spiritual growth in John 17:1-26. Read over this chapter and imagine how the disciples must have felt as they heard Jesus pray passionately to the Father for them.

The disciples were to love and

encourage one another. John 15:12. There is nothing in the world which gives more comfort than an understanding Christian friend.

They were to abide in His words. John 13:7. To abide in His words means, they were to do and act in the way they had been taught.

They were to remember that they were chosen by the Lord in their ministries and He would help them to fulfill them. John 15:16.

They were to help and encourage one another. John 15:13, John 13:15. This means they were to get in and work unselfishly in aiding one another.

They were to remember that Jesus had gone to prepare a place for them and they would soon be together again. John 14:1-6, John 16:16.

He would not leave them alone but would send the Holy Spirit as a special comforter, teacher and helper. His grace and help would be sufficient for any trial they would face. John 14:16, John 16:13.

Jesus gives His disciples some constructive things to do which will produce assurance in this period of trial. These same principles will work for the new convert today. Notice His instructions:

As a loving, protective parent, Jesus reassured them that everything was alright. He tried to make them see that He must go away so the Holy Spirit would come and be able to aid, bless, help and strengthen them personally, because they would soon enter their world-wide ministries.

FRIDAY
V. WORDS SPOKEN WHICH WILL BRING PEACE

"These things I have spoken unto you, that in me ye might have peace. In the world ye shall have tribulation: but be of good cheer; I have overcome the world." JOHN 16:33.

A.　LIFE IS FILLED WITH TRIBULATIONS

This fact was declared by Job when he said, **"Man, *that is* born of a woman, *is* of few days, and full of trouble." JOB 14:1. (+)** It doesn't matter whether one is saved or lost. Life is short and death is sure. There are problems in this world and in everyone's life. Just because a person gets saved does not exempt him from difficulties and trials which plague the human race. In this world of sickness, problems and death the believer has someone to lean on, look to and find comfort and grace in to help in time of need. God's all-sufficient grace aids, leads and comforts the believer as he lives his life for Christ and makes his way toward his heavenly home.

He will have opposition from the world and attacks from the devil which will cause him additional tribulations. **(+)** As these tribulations come, and they will come, remember the words of Jesus in **JOHN 16:33, "...be of good cheer; I have overcome the world." (+)**

B.   LIFE CAN BE LIVED IN PEACE IN THE MIDST OF TRIBULATIONS
      "...In the world ye shall have tribulation..."JOHN 16:33. That is a statement of fact. There is no way a child of God can live a Christian life and then escape criticism and persecution. Paul boldly proclaimed this fact when he said, **"Yea, and all that will live godly in Christ Jesus SHALL SUFFER persecution." II TIMOTHY 3:12**.

      Many of God's people constantly strive to live and never take any kind of stand which leads to persecution. In so doing, they compromise their convictions and grieve the Holy Spirit. But when a person does what God commands and encounters some type of tribulation he experiences a special joy. Paul said that he suffered the loss of all things and counted it but waste that he might know that special **"... fellowship of his sufferings ..."** Philippians 3:7-10. Peter said, **"Beloved, think it not strange concerning the fiery trial which is to try you, as though some strange thing happened unto you: But REJOICE..." I PETER 4:12-13**.

      Jesus said, **"...in me ye might have peace. In the world ye shall have tribulation: but be of good cheer; I have overcome the world." JOHN 16:33**.

      Paul desired **"...the fellowship of his**

suffering..." **PHILIPPIANS 3:10. (+)**
    Peter said that one can and should rejoice in trials.

    These great examples teach that when we stand for the Lord and do the things which He has commanded, then we will have a special fellowship, peace and joy in tribulation.

C.   LIFE CAN BECOME AN ABUNDANT LIFE THROUGH TRIBULATION
    When people are first saved, they want to have patience and become a better Christian. God answers their prayers by sending tribulation. Because "**...tribulation worketh patience;**" **ROMANS 5:3**.

    They long to be a settled, strong, mature and established Christian. Therefore, God allows suffering to come into their lives. He always gives grace to bear the suffering and has designed the suffering, which the believer endures, to work for His eternal good.

    Peter declares, "**But the God of ALL GRACE, who hath CALLED US UNTO HIS ETERNAL GLORY by Christ Jesus, after that YE HAVE SUFFERED A WHILE, make you perfect, stablish, strengthen, settle** *you*." **I PETER 5:10**.

    People long to be more like Jesus. They want to know more about Him and desire to please Him in their lives. In order to fill this desire, God allows some physical problems or illness to come into their family. Paul gives insight in **II CORINTHIANS 4:16-17**. He said,

"...though our outward man perish, yet the inward *man* is renewed day by day. For our light affliction [problems], which is but for a moment [in the light of eternity], worketh for us a far more exceeding *and* eternal weight of glory [reward];"

Paul declares that God has worked so that "...all things work together for good to them that love God..." ROMANS 8:28.

Jesus has overcome the world.

He has taken the sting and dread out of death.(I Corinthians 15:55).

He promises grace for every occasion. He has promised that he will be with the believer in MATTHEW 28:20 "... alway, *even* unto the end of the world. Amen." It is because of these facts, it is because of these PROMISES that the BELIEVER can have PEACE in the midst of tribulation. (+) "These things I have spoken unto you, that in me ye may have peace ..."

LESSON ONE

MONDAY
WORDS SPOKEN TO PREPARE

1. God _____ unto you as unto _____.
2. They must _____ His teaching and _____ the leading of the Holy Spirit.
3. Jesus is touched with _____ of our infirmities. Heb. 4:15.
4. Jesus _____ and cares about the _____ of every one of His _____.
5. He is a _____ that sticketh _____ _____ ___ _____.

TUESDAY
WORDS TO STIMULATE JOY

1. **"My _____ might remain in you, and that _____ _____ might be full".**
2. The expression, "that my joy might remain" _____ that believer can _____ the joy of salvation.
3. Their _____ have forgotten to tell their _____ about it.
4. Jesus came that the believer could be _____ and _____.
5. Jesus wants His children to be _____.

WEDNESDAY
WORDS TO PROTECT FROM OFFENCES

1. These _____ have I spoken unto you, that ye should not be _____.
2. The new convert cannot even imagine that _____ will ever be _____ or _____.
3. Do not be _____ at the _____ or _____ or rejection of your closest _____ or loved ones.
4. Keep a good attitude and _____, pray for and work with them until they _____.
5. Jesus wanted His disciples to be _____ to these _____ so they could be ready _____ them.

THURSDAY
WORDS SPOKEN AS TENDER PARENT

1. Little children ask _____ which, if answered would completely _____ them.
2. "I have yet many things to say unto you, but you cannot _____ them now."
3. A baby needs to be fed _____ and allowed to grow without _____ or _____.
4. Your _____ may be very _____ to you.
5. In times of _____ do what Paul commanded in _____.

FRIDAY
WORDS TO BRING PEACE

1. Man that is _____ of a woman, is of few days and full of _____.
2. He will have _____ from the _____.
3. Be of good_____, I have _____ the world.
4. Paul desired the _____ of his suffering.
5. It is because of these _____ and _____ that the believer can have _____ in the midst of tribulation.

PERSONAL COMMITMENT

Having studied this lesson on God's concern for His children, I now commit myself to allow that concern for others to be reflected through my life.

Questions to be asked: My Grade _____

_____

Name

DAILY FAITH BUILDER

LESSON TWO

GOD'S COVENANT WITH HIS CHILDREN

Special Thought for the Week

I am God's child and He loves me. He will correct me when I am wrong, but He will never let me down or forsake me.

Daily Declaration

I will strive to be honest and fair with God because His love demands correction if I don't.

CHECK BLOCK AFTER REPEATING

	Mon	Tues	Wed	Thurs	Fri	Sat	Sun
A.M.							
P.M							

Memory Verse

"But the salvation of the righteous *is* of the LORD: *he is* their strength in the time of trouble." PSALM 37:39

LESSON TWO

GOD'S COVENANT WITH HIS CHILDREN

INTRODUCTION: God has made a covenant with several men since He created Adam and Eve in the Garden of Eden. In this lesson, we will examine the covenant He made with His children.

MONDAY
I. THE COVENANT IS IMMUTABLE

A.   STATED AND DEFINED

Covenant means, agreement or testament. (+)

Immutable means, unchangeable or unalterable (+)

Therefore, the covenant God makes with man is unchangeable or unalterable. Paul speaks of God's unchangeable covenant or agreement between Himself and the believers in Hebrews 6:11-20.

"For men verily swear by the greater: and an oath for confirmation *is* to them an end of all strife. Wherein God, willing more abundantly to shew unto the heirs of promise the immutability of his counsel, confirmed *it* by an oath: That by two immutable things, in which *it* *was* impossible for God to lie, we might have a strong consolation, who have fled for

refuge to lay hold upon the hope set before us:" HEBREWS 6:16-18.

In verse 16, Paul gives the reason why men take an oath on the witness stand. It is an oath to confirm that they are telling the truth. He uses this example to point out that God, who cannot lie, is mindful of all of His promises and takes an oath upon His own honor that He is telling the exact truth. God wants mankind to take His word literally and believe Him.

B.   THE FIRST IMMUTABLE FACT

In verse 18, Paul speaks of two immutable or unalterable facts. The first unchangeable fact is that God cannot lie.

God is holy. There is no untruthfulness in God. **(+)** His very nature repels untruthfulness. **HEBREWS 6:18** states that, "*...it was* **impossible for God to lie...**"

TITUS 1:2 declares, **"In hope of eternal life, which God, THAT CANNOT LIE, promised..."**

C.   THE SECOND IMMUTABLE FACT

God knew that mankind had a problem stating the truth. Many times, things get bigger and better with the passing of time. Did you ever notice that the fish has a tendency to get bigger each time the story is repeated? Man overstates the beauty, the opportunity or the difficulty. God wanted man to believe Him. God wanted man to realize that whatever God told them was exactly accurate. So,

He states the two immutable principles. The first immutable fact is that God cannot lie. The second immutable or unchangeable fact is that God went to the trouble of taking an oath upon His honor that He was in full control of His understanding when He gave each promise. HE WILL keep each one of them to the most minute detail.

- **First, God cannot lie or overstate. (+)**

- **Second, God took an oath that He was telling the truth when He made each promise. (+) The immutable God WANTS MAN TO BELIEVE HIM!**

TUESDAY
II. THE COVENANT IS BETWEEN TWO PARTIES

A.   GOD MADE THE COVENANT

There are many places in the word of God where He deals with man and makes an agreement with him. Perhaps the plainest chapter which deals with God's covenant is Psalm 89. **(+)** Notice some of His exact statements in this chapter.

"I have made a covenant with my chosen, I have sworn unto David my servant," PSALM 89:3

"My mercy will I keep for him for evermore, and my COVENANT shall stand fast with him." PSALM 89:28(+)

"My covenant will I not break, nor alter the thing that is gone out of my lips." PSALM

89:34

B.   GOD MADE THE COVENANT WITH DAVID

"... I have sworn unto David my servant," God has dealt with many great men in previous generations. **(+)** Adam, Noah, Abraham, Isaac, Jacob, Moses and many others. In Psalm 89, God's attention turns towards the actual physical generation of His son, Jesus. David, a man after His own heart (with one exception) was chosen to be the father of that generation. **(+)** The immutable God makes a covenant which contains several promises to His friend, David.

C.   GOD MADE A COVENANT WITH DAVID'S SEED

This declaration is clearly stated in **PSALM 89:4. "Thy seed will I establish for ever, and build up thy throne to all generations. Selah." (+)** Again, God says the same thing in verses 29 and 36. The seed referred to here are His spiritual descendants, or, the ones who received Christ as their personal Saviour and are born into God's family.

WEDNESDAY
III. THE COVENANT IS CONDITIONAL

God uses the term covenant, or contract, to denote a truth He wanted mankind to understand, because every adult has entered into a contract or agreement with another person or persons. **(+)**

He may have agreed with his father to cut

the lawn when he was a little boy. **(+)** He may have entered a contract with a department store to buy an appliance. He may have engaged an attorney to draw a legal agreement in which party number one was to meet certain conditions with party number two, who then would perform certain feats. But regardless of what agreements he may have entered into, everyone has knowledge of a covenant and how it works.

A. **PARTY NUMBER ONE ENTERS INTO A COVENANT WITH PARTY NUMBER TWO (+)**

In this covenant party number one is God, while number two is the sinner. **(+)** Party number one (God) proclaims to party number two (sinner) that if he will do certain things He, party number one, will forgive him of all his sins and save him from hell.

One should think about the following conditions between party number one (God) and party number two (sinner) in the same way he would if he was entering into a contract to buy a new car. Remember, the immutable God of heaven who cannot lie is the one who is entering into the agreement with the sinner.

B. **THE CONDITIONS WHICH PARTY NUMBER TWO MUST MEET**

Let us consider some of the conditions which the immutable God set down for party number two to meet. Notice the conditions which are set down in **JOHN 5:24**. The verse begins with the expression,

"Verily, verily..." or Truly, truly.

When Jesus begins a verse with this double affirmative, He wants the readers to be doubly aware that He is about to state a truth which is worth attention. He means for the reader to stop and pay strict attention to the statement which is about to be made. **"Verily, verily, I say unto you, He that heareth my word, and believeth on him that sent me, hath everlasting life, and shall not come into condemnation; but is passed from death unto life."**

Hear; man is a sinner.

Hear; God loves sinners and has paid for their sin by sacrificing Jesus on the cross.

Hear; if a sinner will turn from his sins, confess them to God and plead mercy, God will save him.

Believe means believe it and act upon that faith by receiving Jesus as one's personal Saviour.

Those are the only two conditions which the immutable God sets down for the sinner to meet. Hear the message and believe or accept it.

Notice the conditions and promises in **JOHN 10:27-29**, **"My sheep** [saved people] **hear my voice, and I know them, and they follow me: And I give unto them eternal life; and they shall never perish, neither shall any** *man* **pluck them out of my hand. My Father, which gave** *them* **me, is greater than all; and no** *man* **is able to pluck** *them* **out of my Father's hand."** Again, the condition of hearing is clearly stated, **"My sheep hear my voice ..."** The second condition, believing, is implied.

C.   THE PROMISES WHICH PARTY NUMBER ONE MAKES

Notice, in John 5:24, the promises which God makes to the sinner if he meets the two conditions of hearing and believing.

> **Give him everlasting life, "... hath everlasting life ..."**

> **He will not be brought into condemnation or judgment.**

> **He will be brought into a new relationship with God. He "... is passed from death** [separation form God] **unto life** [born into his family]**."**

Notice the promises which He gave the sinner in John 10:27-29

> **"... I give unto them eternal life ..."**

> **"... they shall never perish ..."** (that is, never go to hell)

> **No man can take him from me - "... neither shall any** *man* **pluck them out of my hand."**

If party number two meets the condition which party number one sets, then party number one must perform what he promised party number two. The story is told of two good preacher friends who held different religious convictions on the security of the saved. They would discuss their difference each time they got together. One day, the preacher who believed the sinner was saved as long as he held onto God, but when he turned loose of God and disobeyed Him became lost, tried to make his point in a vivid way. As he rode on his horse under a large tree limb, be grabbed the limb. He held on and exclaimed, *"Look, like a sinner, as long as I hold on like this and do what the Lord commands, I am saved. But, when I turn loose, I fall."* With that, he turned loose of the limb and fell sprawling in the dust.

His preacher friend had noticed a hollow place in the limb. He pointed to the hollow place and said, *"Friend, if you were resting in the hollow place of the limb, you wouldn't fall."*

"That's pretty good," his friend answered. *"Do you have another one?"*

"Yes," came the answer as the man pulled a silver dollar out of his pocket. *"Do you see this silver dollar? If I placed it in that keg* (pointing to a keg setting next to a rain barrel) *and sealed the keg up, then placed the keg in that barrel and sealed up the barrel, how would you get the dollar?"*

"I'd have to break the barrel, take out the

keg, break the keg, and I'd have the dollar."

"That dollar represents the sinner. The keg represents Jesus. The barrel represents God and God is in heaven. Before the devil could get my soul he would have to ascend into heaven, overpower God, and then overpower Jesus."

"That's pretty good, friend," came the reply, *"that's pretty good!"*

"That's not pretty good, my dear brother." came the old pastor's final remark. *"That's Bible."* Then he quoted John 10:27-30.

THURSDAY
IV. THE COVENANT IS BROKEN

A. THE REAL ISSUE

The real issue, which most people struggle with, is, what happens when man sins and breaks his end of the covenant? **(+)** First, may the author confess that man certainly does sin against God. But I have never met any person who was really saved who ceased believing in Jesus as their Saviour.

B. GOD SWORE THAT HE WOULD NOT ALTER HIS COVENANT

Read His exact statement. **"My covenant will I not break, nor alter the thing that is gone out of my lips. Once have I sworn by my holiness that I will not lie unto David." PSALM 89:34-35.**

C.   MAN BREAKS HIS WORD AND SINS

Note the provision in the covenant which covers the condition of man sinning and breaking his agreement. God knew that man would break his end of the agreement. Speaking of David's spiritual children or saved people:

> **"If his children forsake my law, and walk not in my judgments; If they break my statutes, and keep not my commandments;" PSALM 89:30-31**

That is a four-fold breaking of the covenant.

> **Forsook God's law** (did not keep God's laws).

> **Walked not in God's judgments**—walk not IN but outside the judgment of God

> **If they break God's statutes** (written laws).
> **Keep not God's commandments.**

God does not leave anything uncovered. What if they forsake, walk not, break, and keep not...

D.   PARTY NUMBER ONE PROMISES TO PUNISH

God's answer to what happens when one of His children breaks His laws and sins is found in **PSALM 89:32**. *If they FORSAKE, WALK NOT, BREAK AND KEEP NOT;* **(+)** **"Then will I** [God]

visit their transgression with the rod, and their iniquity with stripes."

"They are my children and I am their father. I will deal with them in the same way a loving father deals with his children when they do wrong. **(+)** *I will whip! I will chastise"* but note what he adds to this statement of whipping in the following verse. **(+)**

"Nevertheless my [God's] **lovingkindness will I not utterly** [completely] **take from him** [the one who sinned], **nor suffer my** [God's] **faithfulness to fail."**

God is saying, I will chastise my children and correct them when they sin, but I will not break my covenant. I promised the sinner eternal life. I promised him that he would never perish. I promised him that he would not come into judgment. Just because man lies to me and breaks his agreement and sins, I will not break my covenant (verse 34) with him. I will not lie (verse 35). I will keep my covenant with him and fulfill my promises. **(+)**

FRIDAY
V. THE COVENANT BEARS FRUIT

A. THE COVENANT GIVES CLARITY

God uses terms which the human race can understand. **(+)** When two parties enter an agreement and each perform the required obligations then justice demands each agreement be honored.

The immutable God, in a covenant with David, clarifies the conditions and the effect of meeting conditions. He boldly declares, if a sinner hears and believes then He promises to save and keep that sinner from ever going to hell. In the legal realms, God would be obligated to perform what He promised man that He would do if that sinner met the conditions of hearing and believing. **(+)**

B.   THE COVENANT GIVES CONFIDENCE

When the sinner meets the conditions he is born into God's family. He becomes God's child and from that point God deals with him as a father deals with his son.

If a son fails through weakness, his father is there to lift him up and re-establish his going.

If the son suffers heartbreak, then his father is there to comfort and give grace. If the son sins, the father is there to help his child see the error of his way and turn him back into the path of righteousness. **(+)**

If the son rebels, then his father meets the rebellion with whatever severity is necessary. **(+)** Even in the case of the sin unto death, where God takes the son's physical life. God promises never to leave or forsake His child and this promise gives his children tremendous confidence.

C.   THE COVENANT GIVES COMFORT

There is nothing greater to a son than to have DAD in his corner. **(+)** Your heavenly Father, who saved you, will keep you and help you in every trial. He **"...is a friend *that* sticketh closer than a brother." PROVERBS 18:24** Oh, my dear little brother, you will never have to face the dark dawn alone. The devil may deceive a lost person into sinning, which will destroy him. But God's word states, **"...greater is he that is in you, than he that is in the world."** Through God's grace the son can overcome anything. The fact that we are God's children and are secure gives tremendous confidence and comfort.

This knowledge does not give the child of God a license to sin, because God, his father, will punish His disobedient son.

In this comfort and security the son is able to grow into spiritual maturity and thus fulfill God's plan and purpose for his life. He can proclaim as did David, **"...THOU *ART* my father, my God, and the rock of my salvation." PSALM 89:26**

The covenant which God made is very simple. God said, "Sinner, I will forgive and save you from hell if you will turn from your sin and confess it and forsake it while receiving my Son as your Saviour. When you believe, you are born into My family and become My child. From that moment on I will deal with you as a father deals with a child. If you need help, I will help you. If you need strength, I will give you strength. I will never leave or forsake you. If you sin, I will not overlook it, but will correct you. If you rebel, I will deal more severely with you. I may even take your physical life, but I promised you eternal life and a home in heaven. I will never let anyone take you from Me or suffer you to be lost again and go to hell."

The condition which God lays down to the sinner:

Hear the message of salvation and believe (accept it) the promises which God makes to the sinner;

I will give you eternal life.

I will see to it that you never go to hell.

If you backslide and sin—I will whip and correct you; but I will never forsake you.

Sinner, this loving God would like to enter into this eternal covenant with you also — if you will only with your heart—believe!

LESSON TWO

MONDAY
GOD'S COVENANT IS IMMUTABLE

1. Covenant   means   _____   or _____.
2. Immutable   means   _____   or unalterable.
3. God is _____. There is _____ guile or _____ in God.
4. First_____ can not _____ or overstate.
5. Second God took _____ _____ that he was telling the _____ when he made each _____.

TUESDAY
THE COVENANT IS BETWEEN
TWO PARTNERS

1. Perhaps the _____ _____ which deals with God's _____ is Psalm 89.
2. My covenant will _____ _____ _____ nor alter the thing that is gone out of _____ _____.
3. God has dealt with _____ _____ _____ in previous generations.
4. David was chosen to be the _____ of that generation.
5. Thy _____ will I establish _____.

WEDNESDAY
THE COVENANT IS CONDITIONAL

1. God uses the _____ covenant or contract to denote a truth which he wants mankind to _____.
2. He may have _____ with his father to cut the _____.
3. Party number one enters into a _____ with party number two.
4. Party number one is _____.
5. Party number two is _____ _____.

THURSDAY
THE COVENANT IS BROKEN

1. What happens when man_____ and _____ his end of the covenant?
2. What if they _____, walk not, break and _____?
3. I will _____ with them in the same way a loving _____ deals with his _____.
4. I will _____. I will _____.
5. I will keep _____ _____ with him and_____ my promises.

FRIDAY
THE COVENANT BEARS FRUIT

1. God uses _____ which the human race can _____.
2. In the legal _____ God would be

obligated to _____ what he promised.

3.   The _____ is there to help him see the
       _____ of his way.
4.   His father meets the rebellion with what ever
       _____ necessary.
5.   There is nothing great for a _____
       than to have _____ in his corner.

PERSONAL COMMITMENT

I now recommit my life to the covenant I made with
my Heavenly Father when He saved me.

Date: _____

Questions to be asked: My Grade _____

_____

Name

DAILY FAITH BUILDER

LESSON THREE

GOD'S CLAIM TO HIS CHILDREN

Special Thought for the Week

God made me so I could live my life for HIM.

Daily Declaration

God's claims to me are absolute: He created me, redeemed me and now sustains me; therefore, I am HIS!

CHECK BLOCK AFTER REPEATING

	Mon	Tues	Wed	Thurs	Fri	Sat	Sun
A.M.							
P.M.							

Memory Verse

"For ye are bought with a price: therefore glorify God in your body, and in your spirit, which are God's." I CORINTHIANS 6:20

LESSON THREE

GOD'S CLAIM TO HIS CHILDREN

INTRODUCTION: In this lesson we will show that God has every right to the love, loyalty and full surrender of His children. Giving God first place in one's life is the wisest thing a believer can do. This is especially true when one considers two facts: God has a perfect plan for each of his children's lives and the believer will spend all eternity with God.

MONDAY
I. HIS CLAIM BY RIGHT OF CREATION

A.   THE LOGICAL DEDUCTION

There are only two major theories presented in attempt to explain the origin of the world and mankind—the theory of evolution and the Bible's account of creation. A famous mathematician said that the likelihood of this world and all of its vast, varied and beautiful creatures coming into its present state from a single one-cell creature is about as likely as an explosion in a print shop producing the Webster's Unabridged Dictionary.

The second theory is not only Biblical but is sound scientifically and logically. **(+)**

The author would like for the reader to forget

the Bible for a minute and use his brain and reason with him. It is logical, when one views this vast world, to believe that there was a supernatural being who created it. It is more reasonable to believe that someone designed and created this beautiful and complex world than it is to believe that this world came into existence through an accident.

If this is true, and there is a God...

If that God created man, He must have done so FOR A PURPOSE.

If He made man FOR A PURPOSE, there must be some book or communications from that God which informs man of that purpose.

If God made man for a purpose there must be a day in which that man must stand before his Creator and give account as to how he fulfilled that purpose.

The theory of evolution offers no answers; just questions. The inspired Word God gives answers. It states that:

God made man.

God's inspired Bible is the medium which reveals man's purpose

Man will stand before that God in judgment and give account of how he fulfilled that purpose.

It is because of rebellion toward God that

man invented and now fosters the dumb, blasphemous theory of evolution. Rebellious man does not want to be submissive and subject to a higher power so he invents a method of explaining how this world originated through the unfounded theory of evolution.

B.   THE PLAIN DECLARATION

There is no argument on God's part to try and prove there is a God and that atheism is wrong.

God simply states, **"The fool hath said in his heart, *There is* no God..."** PSALM 14:1 One can search the Bible from cover to cover and never find any other treatment of atheism. God marks him down as a fool and leaves it there. The Bible declares in **GENESIS 1:1**, **"IN the beginning God..."** If one can believe that, then the rest of the Bible is simple. **(+)** There is no event, miracle or happening in the Bible beyond the wisdom and power of God. If there is a God big enough to create this vast universe then the simple little miracles of the Bible are easy to accept. If one cannot accept, **"In the beginning God..."**, then it would be futile to argue the rest of the Bible with him.

Genesis 1:26-27 states boldly—God made man. **JOHN 1:1-3** plainly says, **"In the beginning was the Word, and the Word was with God, and the Word was God. The same was in the beginning with God. All things were made by him; and without him was not anything made that was made."**

C.   THE ABSOLUTE DEMAND

God created the heavens and the earth along with Adam and Eve in six literal 24-hour days. He rested on the seventh day, or, Saturday. **(+)**

He commanded mankind to cease his labors and rest on the Sabbath day. Many years later, God gave Israel the Mosaic laws which contained many laws governing the Sabbath day.

In **EXODUS 20:8,** the fourth commandment clearly states, **"Remember the sabbath day, to keep it holy."** The Jews weren't allowed to travel over one mile (Sabbath day's journey) on the Sabbath. **(+)** They were not to work at all. The Bible records the stoning of disobedient and rebellious Sabbath day breakers.

Why, the reader may question, was there such severe treatment for breaking the Sabbath day?

The reason! God gave the commandment of keeping the Sabbath day to teach mankind that they belong to God. **(+)**

God made man.

He made man for a purpose. Man was to stop everything—take one day—teach his children about the great God who had made man. He was to teach His children about the purpose for man's existence on the earth. He was to teach His children how Adam had sinned against God and became separated from God. He was to teach His children that they were eternal, that God loved them; that

God had made provisions for man's reconciliation to Himself; how to worship properly and how to prepare to spend eternity with God. The Sabbath day was given to remind man that he belongs to God by virtue of creation.

TUESDAY
II. HIS CLAIM BY RIGHT OF REDEMPTION

A.   THE POSSESSION BECAME LOST

"And God saw every thing he had made, and, behold, *it was* very good..." GENESIS 1:31. The man He had made lived in a beautiful paradise with his beautiful bride and was in complete harmony with both his surroundings and his creator.

God warned Adam about sin and death. **(+)** But the devil in his subtlety used woman to cause Adam to rebel against God and sin!

The beautiful relationship which Adam enjoyed with his God was marred by sin and paradise was LOST. **(+)** Sin, death and the devil with all their plagues have pursued mankind ever since.

B.   THE PRICE OF REDEMPTION

Adam, **"...the fruit of the tree *which* is in the midst of the garden, God hath said, Ye shall not eat of it, neither shall ye touch it, lest ye die... ...the soul that sinneth, it shall die... ...the wages of sin *is* death..." GENESIS 3:1; EZEKIEL 18:4; ROMANS 6:23**

The just, holy, righteous God of heaven, if He is to have fellowship with sinful, rebellious man again, must somehow satisfy His broken law.

But, the demand of the broken law is death; physical, mental and spiritual death. It was very clear to God. There is only one way to redeem lost, fallen man. I must pay for his sin by giving my Son to die in his place as his substitute.

For a wife and family, a man might die; for a country and a cause, some would give their lives; but to die for his enemies...

To become sinful...

For the Son of God to take upon Himself man's sin and actually take the place of and become rebellious, ungodly, sorted, perverted man;...

For God's only begotten Son to have broken fellowship with His Father, to be hated and totally abandoned by both God and man—in order to buy back, to redeem, to restore lost, fallen man! No wonder God turned His back—no wonder the sun hid its face—no wonder the earth quaked—when Jesus, the Son of God, became sin and hung on the cross as the sinner's substitute. Such agony which stemmed from such love as Jesus manifested on the cross as He redeemed and made a way for lost man to be reconciled with the Creator by sacrificing Himself in that sinner's place. THE SAVED BELONG TO GOD BY RIGHT OF REDEMPTION.

C.   THE PLAIN CLAIM OF OWNERSHIP

In **I CORINTHIANS 6:19**, Paul begins the verse by saying, **"What?"** as if he was startled or surprised. **(+)** It is as if he could not believe he had to inform the carnal Christians of the Corinthian church of the next truth. Then he asked them a second question, **"...know YE NOT that your body is the temple of the Holy Ghost *which IS* IN YOU, which ye have of God, and YE ARE NOT YOUR OWN?"**

Don't you know that you are not your own? Hasn't that fact dawned upon you? Then he boldly stated in **verse 20, "For YE are BOUGHT WITH A PRICE: THEREFORE** [because of this] **GLORIFY GOD in your body, and in your spirit, WHICH ARE GOD'S."** **(+)** Peter said, **"Forasmuch as ye know that ye were not REDEEMED** [bought back from the slave market] **with corruptible things... But with the precious BLOOD OF CHRIST..." (+) I Peter 1:18-19.** The believer belongs to God, because God bought and paid for him through the sacrifice of His Son.

WEDNESDAY
III. HIS CLAIM BY RIGHT OF MAINTENANCE

God not only owns you by right of creation, but He purchased you by giving His only begotten Son to redeem you.

But God has a stronger claim on your life. He gave you your very life. **JOHN 1:9** states that He **"...lighteth every man that cometh into the world."** Paul wrote, **"...by him all things consist." COLOSSIANS 1:17.** Consist comes from the Greek word which means *"held together"* or *"maintained."* **(+)**

In a sermon which Paul preached on Mars Hill He proclaimed, **"For in him we live, and move, and have our being..."** ACTS 17:28

Daniel told the wicked king, Belshazzar, that his very *"breath"* was in the hand of God. Daniel 5:23

From these verses we learn that God gives us our life and the very energy to breathe and to move about. Man cannot, by conscious thought, add one cubit to his stature (Matthew 6:27). **(+)** There is not one bird that dies without God's knowledge (Matthew 10:29) and yet He maintains and holds this vast universe together. You belong to this powerful God because He gives and sustains your very existence. He keeps your heart beating and your lungs breathing. He keeps you alive when you go into unconscious sleep each night. David declared, **"Thou preparest a table before me in the presence of mine enemies..."** Psalm 23:5. You belong to God because He gives you life.

A.   THERE IS A PRESCRIBED WAY FOR YOU TO WALK

He saved you for a purpose (II Timothy 1:9) and has ordained the lifestyle and work you are to perform for Him. **"For we are his workmanship, created in Christ Jesus unto good works, which God hath before ORDAINED that we should walk in them."** EPHESIANS 2:10 When one is in the will of God there is a hedge built around him which protects him from evil (Job 1:10). God sent Paul into the dangers, but assured him that he would keep him safe (Acts 26:17). He promised **"...all things work together for good to them that love God, to them who are the called according to *his* purpose." ROMANS 8:28**.

The Bible tells us in John 10:10, Jesus came that the believer might live the abundant life. Paul beseeched the Romans to, **"...prove what *is* that GOOD, and ACCEPTABLE, and PERFECT, will of God." ROMANS 12:2**. My little brother, God has a perfect plan and will for your life.

B. THERE ARE DANGERS OUTSIDE THE PRESCRIBED WILL OF GOD

Note the sad commentary of some who refused to follow in lawful paths. Some made shipwreck of their lives and were delivered unto Satan. I Timothy 1:20. **(+)** Paul wept over some and said they had become enemies of the Cross of Christ. Philippians 3:18. Some refused to live by faith and **"...drew back unto perdition [destruction] ..." Hebrews 10:39**.

Some forsook their preacher and turned back to the world. II Timothy 4:10.

Some became sick, while others died because they would not examine themselves and repent. I Corinthians 11:30-32.

Some died broken-hearted with the blood of their very children on their hands. Psalms 51:14, II

Samuel 18:33.

The devil caused Peter to swear and deny Jesus.

King David was out of the will of God when he looked, lusted and committed his infamous sins.

A man who will not yield his life fully to Jesus is certainly subjecting himself and his family to the possibility of untold heartaches and dangers.

C.   THERE IS A NEED FOR PREPARATION

In order to know the will of God and have the spiritual strength to do it, one must prepare himself spiritually and walk within God's ordained framework. This preparation should begin in the home as soon as the child is born.

God's ordained plan is for the father to be the spiritual leader of his home and train his children. (+) Too many parents depend too heavily upon taking the family to Sunday School so *"the church can teach them."* Many parents feel they have done their religious duty when they have done this. Other parents have turned their kids over to a youth department or to a Christian school.

The church is to undergird what the parent teaches at home and provide a place for fellowship, but God's plan has not changed. The parents are to train their children at home. The Bible clearly commands the parent, **"Train up a child in the way he should go: and when he is old, he will not depart from it." PROVERBS 22:6**.

Listen to the forceful command of God which has not changed. **"...THESE WORDS, WHICH I COMMAND THEE..." DEUTERONOMY 6:6** He did not say, put them on a Sunday School bus or turn them over to some church, or even enroll them in a Christian School. But Dad, look what He did say. **"...thou shalt teach them diligently unto thy children..." DEUTERONOMY 6:7**. WHERE ARE THE PARENTS TO TEACH THEIR CHILDREN? Parents are to talk to them,

"...when thou sittest in thine house..."

"...when thou walkest by the way..."

"...when thou liest down..."

"...when thou risest up..."

In verses eight and nine he further instructs the fathers on their personal responsibility and how to instruct their children. In verse 10 and 11, he reminds them of God's great goodness to them. But in **verse 12** he severely warns, **"...beware lest thou forget the Lord..."**

God has not changed in His place of training children nor has He changed in His method. **(+)** He still requires ONE DAY PER WEEK TO BE SET ASIDE FOR THAT PURPOSE.

THE LORD'S DAY IS SUNDAY.

In the Old Testament, it was Saturday. The Jews were to honor His Lordship and to remember they belonged to God by ceasing work and teaching their children about holy (God's) things every Sabbath day. If Saturday was a special day to the people of Old Testament times, then how much more should we show respect for Sunday. It only cost God a little energy to create man. It cost Him His Son to redeem man. The saints of God are to assemble themselves upon the first day of the week in commemoration of the resurrection of Jesus Christ from the dead. When a family sets aside Sunday to remember the love, the suffering, the purchasing of their soul and family from the powers of sin and the dangers of hell, then they will develop a proper foundation for Christian growth and will be well on their way in serving Christ successfully.

THURSDAY
IV. HIS CLAIM BY RIGHT OF LORDSHIP

We belong to God because He created us.

We belong to God because He gives us breath and life.

We belong to God because we voluntarily agreed to the purchase price which God gave to redeem us from hell.

Since those three statements are true, what should our attitude be toward God? **(+)**

A. BEHAVIOR IN THE LIGHT OF LORDSHIP

Paul declares, "**Moreover it is required in stewards, that a man be found faithful.**" **(+) I CORINTHIANS 4:2**. A steward is a person who watches over and cares for the property of another. We are not our own, we belong to God. We are simply stewards over ourselves, our children, our time, our influence and our possessions. The things which God has given into our care we should manage for His benefit and glory.

Our attitude toward our children should be the same as Hannah's attitude toward her son, Samuel, when she gave him back to God. Read the account of Hannah's stewardship in I Samuel 1:12-28. Then read one of the greatest declarations of joy and triumph found in the Bible in I Samuel 2:1-10. This came from the heart of a woman who realized that her son was a gift from God to be given back to Him in Christian service. Contrast the joy of Hannah with the frustration which most mothers experience as they try to raise their sons to be successful in this world.

B. BEHAVIOR WHICH RECOGNIZES HIS LORDSHIP

Our primary purpose is to get the Gospel out to the people of the world. Matthew 28:29; Mark 16:15; John 20:21.

We are to lay up treasures in heaven and not on this earth. Matthew 6:19.

We are not to be conformed (live like) to this world's standards but be transformed (make like) and live the Christ-like standard life. Romans 12:2.

We are to set our "...**affection on things above, not on things on the earth.**"

COLOSSIANS 3:1-2. We are to put down the fleshly, human desires. Colossians 3:5-9.

Women should always dress modestly which would identify them as Christian women. If there is any doubt, don't wear it. I Timothy 2:9-10.

Men should always remember that they were created in the image of God. Paul said that long hair was a shame to a man. I Corinthians 11:14. He strongly denounced the practice of a man being effeminate (acting more like a woman than a man). I Corinthians 6:9-10. A man should imitate the example of dedicated Christian leaders in their hair style instead of following the hair style of the world.

We belong to God. We are to dress like, talk like, look like, and live like we belong to God in our daily behavior.

C. BEHAVIOR WHICH HINDERS GOD'S BLESSING AND PURPOSE

Many preachers preach on separation from the world in a cold, legal, intolerant way. Their attitude in their preaching is critical and harsh. Many Christians are repulsed or turned off by these preachers more by their intolerant attitude than by what they preach. **(+)** May the author urge you to consider living a separated life from the world for two outstanding reasons:

Live a separated life from the world in order to get your prayers answered. **(+)** In II Corinthians 6:14, Paul said the child of God should not be unequally yoked (coupled) with the unbeliever. After giving other examples in verses 14-16, in **verse 17** he commands the believer to **"...come out from among them, and be ye separate...and touch not the unclean** *thing*..." When the Christian meets these conditions God can really help them in their lives. The beloved disciple declares, **"And whatsoever we ask, we receive of him, because we keep his commandments, and do those things that are pleasing in his sight." I John 3:22**. If we are a friend of the world then we are displeasing to God and actually hinder his work. In our failure to live a separated life from the world we hinder our own prayers from being answered.

We should live a separated life from the world for testimony sake. When we get saved everyone begins to observe our actions. The rest watch to see if there is a change in our life. They cannot see our heart so they have to depend on what we say, how we live, our attitude and our outward disposition. They watch where we go and how we act. We become their Bible. II Corinthians 3:2. They read our lives. We should not engage in questionable practices but rather abstain from anything which does not honor and glorify God. Paul said,

"**Whether therefore ye eat, or drink, or whatsoever ye do, DO ALL TO THE GLORY OF GOD." I CORINTHIANS 10:31(+)** We should live a separated life from the world in order to manifest that salvation is real and to back up our testimony. In doing so, we will win our family and friends to Christ.

V. HIS CLAIM BY RIGHT OF FUTURE

COMPANIONSHIP

The end of this short, brief journey on this earth will expand into the vastness of eternity with God. **(+)** He made us, He sustains us, He has redeemed us and soon He will receive us home.

A mother once admonished her fine, upright son who was leaving home to serve his country in the army. *"Son, while you are gone away from home, do not do anything or get involved in anything which you cannot tell your father about when you get home."*

That would be a tremendous philosophy for a child of God to live by as he makes his way toward his eternal Father and home.

A. WELL DONE, THOU GOOD AND FAITHFUL SERVANT(+)

In Matthew 25:14-30, we have the parable (story) of a man who left his property and took a journey into a far country. Before leaving he called his three servants and gave them responsibilities over his property. He gave five talents to one servant, two talents to another and one talent to the third. When he returned from his journey, he (reckonth) judged them. The one who had five talents had gained five additional talents while the second servant had gained two additional talents. The master told them both, **"...Well done, *thou* good and faithful servant: thou hast been faithful over a few things, I will make thee ruler over many things: enter thou into the joy of thy lord."** Verse 21. The servant who had received one talent, **"...digged in the earth** [worldly minded], **and hid his lord's money."** Verse 18. These first two servants represent the faithful children of God who worked for Christ and who were faithful stewards. The Bible teaches that the faithful will become heirs with Christ (Romans 8:17) and rule and reign with him for a thousand years on earth (II Timothy 2:12). **"...have thou authority over ten cities. And the second came...he said likewise to him, Be thou also over five cities." LUKE 19:17-19**.

B.   THOU   WICKED   AND   SLOTHFUL SERVANT

The servant who hid his Lord's money and said, **"...Lord, I knew thee that thou art an hard man...And I was afraid, and went and hid thy talent..." MATTHEW 25:24-25**.

"His Lord answered and said unto him, ***Thou*** **wicked and slothful servant...Take therefore the talent from him...and cast ye the unprofitable servant into outer darkness: there shall be weeping and gnashing of teeth." (verse 26-30**).

Keep in mind that Jesus is illustrating (**"...*kingdom of heaven IS* AS..." verse 14**) a spiritual truth. There were three servants. Each of these three servants called their master **"Lord"** and when they were addressed by their master the reference started **"His Lord"**.

Two of these servants were faithful and were rewarded. One of the servants was unfaithful and was rebuked by **"His Lord"**.

The expression, **"...there shall be weeping and gnashing of teeth."** confuses some because this expression in other passages of scripture refers to those who are suffering in hell. Cast ye the unprofitable who? Is the word servant or sinner? We have already noticed that the sinner when saved is given eternal life and has God's word that he will never perish or go to hell.

Please keep in mind that the subject under consideration is rewards. It is not salvation. When Jesus returns He will judge and reward His servants (Rev. 22:12). The Judgment of the lost will take place 1,000 years later. (We will study the time of these judgments in later lessons).

Just because there will be **"...weeping and gnashing of teeth."** does not mean that the person has gone to hell. There have been many people who realized the fearful consequence of some careless deed which cost a life (or some horrible accident) and have wept and gritted or gnashed their teeth.

"...cast ye the unprofitable servant into outer darkness..." does not mean the person goes to hell.

In studying the symbolic language in the Bible it is clear that light symbolized God, life and fellowship with God in Righteousness. Darkness symbolizes the world, sin and DISFELLOWSHIP with God. Note the language in **EPHESIANS 5:8-13 "For ye were sometimes darkness, but now *are*** *ye* **light in the Lord: walk as children of light... And have no fellowship with the unfruitful works of darkness, but rather reprove** *them***... But all things that are reproved are made manifest by the light: for whatsoever doth make manifest is light.**"

"Ye [saved] **are the light of the world...**" **MATTHEW 5:14**
A strong verse which teaches that light represents fellowship with God and darkness represent non-fellowship with God is **I JOHN 1:6-7**. **"If we say that we have FELLOWSHIP with him, and walk in darkness, we lie, and do not the truth: But if we walk in the light, as he is in the light, we have FELLOWSHIP one with another...**" One can lose fellowship with his father but he can not lose sonship.

The faithful servants will enter into the joy of the Lord and reign with him during the 1,000 year millennium reign.

The unfaithful servant was not cast into hell, but was exposed as an unfaithful, untrustworthy servant and placed with the rest of the worldly, undedicated Christians who will be ruled over by Christ during the 1,000 year reign. In the 1,000 year reign on the earth, the faithful will fellowship with Christ and walk in the light of his love. **(+)** The unfaithful servants will not reign with Christ during the 1,000 years, but will be reigned over. **(+)** Their works will be burned (I Cor. 3:13).

In Revelation 21:4, the Bible states that God will wipe away all tears. Then it states that the former things are passed away or forgotten.

But, dear friend, these statements are made after the 1,000 year reign is over. These statements are made after the great White Throne Judgment, when the lost hear their doom pronounced and are cast into the lake of fire or the final eternal hell.

This verse seems to teach the possibility of the unfaithful servant living the complete 1,000 years with the full realization of what his unfaithful, slothful life did to the cause of Christ.

If these dear people lived with the memory of their past sins, their lost loved ones in hell, the scorching denunciation of Christ, and the fact that they were worldly, unfaithful servants who hindered people instead of helping them, then this knowledge would cause them to weep. It would cause them to grind their teeth.

If their tears are not wiped away until after the 1,000 years is over and they must live with the haunting memories of a misspent life then it would explain the expression of "weeping and gnashing of teeth." We know that God is going to wipe away all tears and the former things will pass away (Rev. 21:4), before we enter the eternal, heaven age. But, I must confess that all evidence that I have ever found in the scripture makes me believe that unfaithful saints will go through the 1,000 years on this earth with their minds very much aware of their past lives. Jesus has openly rebuked them as slothful servants. They have not been rewarded. Their works have been burned and they are saved so as by fire.

The child of God should not take any chances on what these verses mean. He should faithfully "work out" his salvation with "fear and trembling". Not only will the behavior of the saved affect the position during the 1,000 year reign, but many of the rewards that the saved receive for faithful dedicated service will last beyond the millennium, they will be enjoyed eternally. **(+)**

As the child of God makes his way through life it certainly behooves him to live in such a way as to be able to GLADLY TELL HIS FATHER ALL ABOUT HIS JOURNEY WHEN HE GETS HOME.

LESSON THREE

MONDAY
HIS CLAIM BY RIGHT OF CREATION

1. The second theory is not only Biblical but is sound _____ and _____.
2. In the beginning _____ if one can believe that the _____ of the Bible is _____.
3. God created the _____ and the _____ in six _____ 24 hour days.
4. The Jews weren't allowed to travel over _____ mile _____ _____ _____ on the Sabbath.
5. God gave the _____ of keeping the Sabbath to teach mankind that they _____ _____ _____.

TUESDAY
HIS CLAIM BY RIGHT OF REDEMPTION

1. God had _____ Adam about _____ and _____.
2. The beautiful _____ which Adam enjoyed with his God was _____ _____ _____ and paradise was _____.
3. Paul begins the verse by saying, _____ as if he was _____ or surprised.
4. Glorify God in your _____ and in your spirit which _____ _____.

5.   But with the precious _____ of Christ.

WEDNESDAY
HIS CLAIM BY RIGHT OF MAINTAINANCE

1.   Consist comes from a greek word which means, "held _____ _____ _____".
2.   Man _____ _____ by conscious thought add one _____ to his stature.
3.   Some made _____ of their _____ and were delivered over to _____ I Timothy 1:20.
4.   God's ordained plan is for the _____ to be the_____ _____ of his home and _____ his children.
5.   God has not _____ in his place of training _____ nor has he _____ his _____.

THURSDAY
HIS CLAIM BY RIGHT OF LORDSHIP

1.   Since those three statements are true, what should our _____ be toward God?
2.   "Moreover, it is required in _____, that a man be found _____".
3.   Many Christians are _____ or turned off by these preachers more by their _____ _____ than by what they preach.
4.   Live a _____ life from the world in order to get _____ _____ _____.
5.   Whether therefore ye eat, or drink, or

_____ you do, do all to the
_____ _____ _____.

FRIDAY
HIS CLAIM BY FUTURE COMPANIONSHIP

1. This short journey will _____ into the vastness of _____ _____ _____.

2. Well done, thou _____ and _____ servant.

3. In the _____ year reign, the faithful will _____ with Christ.

4. The unfaithful will not _____ with Christ during the 1000 year _____.

5. Many of the _____ for faithful, dedicated service will be enjoyed _____.

PERSONAL COMMITMENT

God being my helper I will live my life under His claims, and strive to glorify him through my life.
.

Date: _____

Questions to be asked: My Grade _____

_____

Name

DAILY FAITH BUILDER

LESSON FOUR

GOD'S COURSE FOR HIS CHILDREN

Special Thought for the Week

The wise man chosen by God to find the very purpose for man's existence stated in **PROVERBS 11:30**, "… **he that winneth souls is wise.**"

Daily Declaration

I will constantly look for an opportunity to share my faith

CHECK BLOCK AFTER REPEATING

	Mon	Tues	Wed	Thurs	Fri	Sat	Sun
A.M.							
P.M							

Memory Verse

"And they that be wise shall shine as the brightness of the firmament: and they that turn many to righteousness as the stars for ever and ever." DANIEL 12:3

LESSON FOUR

GOD'S COURSE FOR HIS CHILDREN

INTRODUCTION: One of the main thoughts which consumed the Apostle Paul's mind was God's course or purpose for his life. **(+)** He told Timothy we were all saved for a purpose. II Timothy 1:9. He consoled the Ephesian pastors when they warned him that if he went to Jerusalem he would suffer bodily harm or even death by saying, **"But none of these things move me, neither count I my life dear unto myself, so that I might finish my COURSE WITH JOY..." ACTS 20:24**. **(+)** One of his last statements of triumph before he was martyred in Rome was, **"...I have finished *my* course [job]..." II TIMOTHY 4:6-8**

MONDAY
I. THE THINGS DONE UNDER THE SUN

One of the primary questions which all men ask is, *"What is this life all about? Why is man on this earth?"* God anticipated man's questions and gave the clear-cut answer in the Bible.

A.   COMISSION OF LIFE

One of the 66 inspired books was written just to answer this question. God chose the wisest, richest and the most supreme ruler of the earth and commissioned him to find the answer to the questions: What is life all about? Why is man on this earth? What will make man happy and give him complete fulfillment in and with his life?

The man's name was King Solomon.

The inspired book in which this question is found is the book of Ecclesiastes. **(+)**

This question is stated in **ECCLESIASTES 1:13** and re-stated in **ECCLESIASTES 2:3**. Solomon testified that he gave himself **"...to seek and search out...all *things* that are done under heaven...till I might see what *was* that good for the sons of men, which they should do under the heaven all the days of their life."** In simple language these verses state that Solomon gave his life to find out for what purpose God placed men on the earth.

B.   COMMITTMENT TO EXPERIMENT

If one would read all the book of Ecclesiastes he would discover it is a series of experiments on the part of King Solomon. Some of the experiments Solomon tried are:

- The lunacy of liquor (or, the emptiness and foolishness of alcohol).
- The ludicrousness of laughter (or living it up).
- The lucid emptiness of luxury (and what money can buy).
- The laborious worriment of labor (or who's going to get what I have).
- The lying lytta of lust (or deceived to despair).

After each experiment, Solomon maintained that man was placed on the earth for a far greater purpose than what he found from the fulfillment in that realm. After each experiment, he would express sadness, emptiness and declare "...all *is* vanity." **ECCLESIASTES 1:2**

C. CONCLUSION OF THE EXPERIMENT

Every scientific experiment demands a conclusion. **(+)** The wisest man on earth gave his findings in Ecclesiastes 12:13-14. In his summary, he gave the general purpose for man's existence on the earth. **(+)** In the book of Proverbs 11:30, he states the purpose for the Child of God's life. His deductions after a lifetime of investigation into the purpose of God's creation of man and why he placed him on the earth are very pointed. Memorize the inspired findings of why you and the rest of the human race are alive as stated by Solomon in **ECCLESIASTES 12:13-14**. **"Let us hear the conclusion of the whole matter: Fear God, and keep his commandments: for this *is* the whole *duty* of man. For God shall bring every work into judgment, with every secret thing, whether *it be* good, or whether *it be* evil."** In the following sections we will give the primary purpose which God has for each believer's life.

II. THE THINGS THE REDEEMED ARE TO DO

Jesus spent 3 ½ years on the earth training leaders. **(+)** After His resurrection and just before His ascension back into Heaven, He reaffirmed what He wanted His disciples to do. These final words are given in what is called the great commission.

We will briefly explain each account of the great commission so one can see the primary work for the saved.

A. THE COMMISSION AS FOUND IN MATTHEW

In Matthew 28:18-20, Jesus told his disciples to go into all the world and disciple people well enough to win and disciple others. The order is, go into each nation of the world, win people, train those won to the level where they can win and train their own people. **(+)**

B. THE COMMISSION AS FOUND IN MARK

In **MARK 16:15,** "**...Go ye into all the world, and preach the gospel to every creature.**" This gives the individual believer a personal responsibility of preaching or telling each person in the believer's world. **(+)**

C. THE COMMISSION AS FOUND IN LUKE

In **LUKE 24:46-49**, the great commission is that the plan of salvation is to be "**...preached in his name among all nations, beginning at Jerusalem.**"

D. THE COMMISSION AS FOUND IN JOHN

In **JOHN 20:21-23**, Jesus tells the believers that their job is the same as His job was while He was living on the earth. "**...as *my* Father hath sent**

me, even so send I you." Jesus came to seek and to save the lost. Jesus concludes the great commission in verse 23 by placing the fearful consequences and responsibilities upon the believers by proclaiming, **"Whose soever sins you remit, they are remitted unto them;** *and* **whose soever** *sins* **you retain, they are retained."** Simply stated, as the believer goes, tells and persuades the sinner to turn from his sins and call upon the name of the Lord; his sins are forgiven or remitted. If the saved do not go, the sinner will not hear, will not turn and will not call upon the name of the Lord so his sins are retained and he dies lost. THE SAVED MUST GO. **(+)**

E.   THE COMMISSION AS FOUND IN ACTS

In Acts 1:8, Jesus said the believer must be empowered by the Holy Spirit in order to become an effective witness. Then he expressly commanded them to get the gospel to every man, woman, boy and girl in every town, nation and continent of the whole world. The last words of Jesus, as recorded in the great commission, to his disciples clearly shows that the saved are to get the gospel to the lost. **(+)** That is the believer's primary charge from God.

WEDNESDAY
III. THE TESTIMONY OF THE GREATS

As we attempt to help the believer understand the primary purpose for his life and what he ought to be doing as a Christian, it is clear that the Lord intended that each saved person was responsible, as an individual believer, to carry the gospel to the lost. Each account of the great commission stresses that the believer is to "go." Consider what some of the great men of the Bible have said on this subject.

A. KING DAVID DECLARED HIS UNDER-STANDING OF HIS PRIMARY PURPOSE.

David had sinned grievously and was uttering his heart-stirring prayer in Psalm 51. He pleaded with God to forgive him of his sins, and restore the joy of salvation. He promised God that if He would renew a right spirit within him and restore the joy of salvation then David would return to his primary purpose and work. He would return to the work of getting sinners saved. Read the declaration of his intent in **PSALM 51:13**. **"*Then*** [based upon God's restoring the joy of salvation to David] **will I teach transgressors thy ways; and sinners SHALL BE CONVERTED unto thee." (+)** David so much as said, *"God if you will forgive me. I'll get back to soul-winning."*

B. THE WISEST MAN WHO EVER LIVED GAVE THIS WISDOM.

"The fruit of the righteous [saved] ***is* a tree of life; and he that winneth souls *is* wise." PROVERBS 11:30. (+)** The man who gave his life to find out why God placed man on this earth so much as declared, *"The people who win souls are the ones who have found the real purpose of life and are wise."*

C. THE MAN WHO WROTE FOURTEEN

BOOKS OF THE NEW TESTAMENT DECLARED

This man was the great Apostle Paul and was saved to become the believer's pattern. (I Timothy 1:16) He said, "**...I am made all things to all _men_, that I MIGHT BY ALL MEANS SAVE SOME.**" in **I CORINTHIANS 9:22. (+)** He told the Ephesians, in **ACTS 20:31,** that during the three years he was their pastor he had warned sinners "**...night and day with tears.**" He also stated that he was "**...pure from the blood of all _men_**" because he had declared "**...all the counsel of God.**" **ACTS 20:26-27**. The examples and writings of Apostle Paul reveal man's purpose; that is, to win souls.

D.   JESUS, THE SON OF GOD, WAS A SOUL-WINNER. (+)

He personally witnessed to and won Nicodemus at night. He won the woman at the well. He called Zacchaeus down from the tree and saved him. He healed and saved the man who lived in the graveyard. He cleansed and saved the woman who was taken in adultery. He prolonged His suffering to save the thief on the cross.

Here and there, everywhere, Jesus went about seeking and saving sinners. He was known as **"a friend of sinners."** He ended His personal ministry by telling the saved, **"As my father sent me** (Luke 19:10) **even so, send I you." (+)** If you follow Jesus, He will make you a fisher of men.

THURSDAY

IV. THE TENDENCY OF THE REDEEMED

A.   TO DISCUSS DOCTRINE

One of the natural tendencies of the believer is to discuss the Bible or talk doctrine. Paul admonished the believer to leave the principles of the doctrine of Christ in Hebrews 6:1. He listed the doctrine that believers discuss and the debate as the world goes to hell. **"And this will we do, if God permit." (verse 3)** which means that believers have a tendency to discuss doctrine and to not go as Jesus commands. **(+)** The subject in this Scriptural setting is, turn away from the empty discussing of the doctrines and go on to maturity or serving Christ in winning souls.

B.   TO DISPLAY OUTWARD FORM OF RELIGION

Another tendency of the religious is to stress the order of service and its program. In Isaiah 1:11-15, God plainly denounced the religious services of the Jews. God said He was sick of their services, that He hated them. **(+)** He said He would hide His face from them and that He would not hear their prayers.

In Isaiah 5:12-14, He said their services were all dried up and were causing people to go to hell. Jesus strongly denounced the formal services of the Pharisees and their stress of tradition. **(+)** He said that their hearts were far from God and their lips uttered empty words. Many fundamental churches are less than one generation from this formalism because they have already stopped their own personal soul-winning.

C.   TO   DISTAIN   PERSONAL
RESPONSIBILITY

Most church "*goers*" love the blessings and the benefits, but it is hard to get them involved. Jeremiah was inspired by the Holy Spirit to charge the Jewish people with the "**…blood of the souls of the poor innocents…**" because they had stopped their soul winning. **JEREMIAH 2:34**. The Jews answered vehemently and declared they had not sinned. *"We have kept ourselves pure from the world, we are normal."* God rejected their arguments and answered, "**…hast thou also taught the wicked ones thy ways." JEREMIAH 2:33**. **(+)** Have you told them how to get to heaven? **(+)** Have you shared the Four Spiritual Principles? Have you preached the Gospel (Good News of God's Love) to them? These Jews distained their personal responsibility of telling the lost about salvation and were themselves rebuked by God and charged with sinner's blood. The saved are to have regular church services but that is not the primary purpose of their lives. Their primary purpose is to win the lost.

FRIDAY
V. THE TEACHING OF JESUS

Most religious leaders and churches have such a blindness toward the fact that the individual child of God is to personally seek out and win souls that Jesus devoted a whole chapter in the Bible to that principle. The chapter is one of the best known in the Bible, **LUKE 15**, but the truth which caused him to write the chapter is still hidden from the majority.

A.   THE SINNERS CAME

In verse 1, the sinners and publicans came to Jesus. They had needs and were convinced that Jesus would help them. This caused the religious crowd to murmur, verse 2. They complained, **"...This man receiveth sinners, and eateth with them."** Because of their lack of understanding of the purpose of Jesus' life and the real reason for having a church, Jesus spake **"...THIS PARABLE..."** verse 3. It does not say these parables, but this parable. The 15th chapter is not made up of three parables, namely; the parable of the lost sheep, lost coin and the prodigal son. It is made up of one parable which shows the purpose for man's life, that of seeking sinners. **(+)**

B.   THE SAINTS CHARGED.

In this parable the conditions of the sinner, the concern of the Saviour and the true commitment of the saved are revealed. The sheep denote the sinner's nature; they go astray and must be sought. The shepherd leaves the sheep who are safe in the fold to seek, find and rescue the lost sheep. The sheep represent the sinner. This truth is stated in verse 7 which gives the punch line of the story when it states, **"...likewise joy shall be in heaven over one sinner that repenteth..."** **(+)**That statement about joy in heaven over the salvation of a sinner, confirms the point that Jesus made is about seeking sinners.

The coin became lost through the act of another. Through one man, Adam, we all became sinners. The coin will not recover itself, it must be sought and found. When the coin was found the neighbors were called and they rejoiced with the woman. Jesus clearly is illustrating the seeking, finding and salvation of the sinner by the Christian. **(+)**

We know this by the clear application Jesus made in verse 10. **"Likewise, I say unto you, there is joy in the presence of the angels of God over one sinner that repenteth."**

C.   THE SERVICES CONFUSED

The sheep denote we are sinners by nature.

The coin shows that we are sinners through the act of another.

The boy manifests that we are sinners by choice.

The father represents God the Father.

The older brother manifests the attitude of a church member who is faithful to the church services but does not realize the main purpose of the church is to see sinners saved. The elder brother heard the rejoicing over the lost sinner, remembered all the work he had done **"...in the field..."** (verse 25) and became upset. This attitude represents the attitude of members who are confused about why we have church services. Many faithful members in a local church have resentment toward the way the pastor makes over the *"Bus Kids"* or the *"long haired hippy"* who professed to be saved. They are loyal to the demonstration. They give to the church, play on the ball team, have fellowship at the church socials, attend most of the services and believe that when they do those things it makes them *"good members"* or *"good Christians."* The elder brother (older church member) told his father how he felt, (verses 29-30). The old father entreated his son by saying in verse 31, **"...Son, thou art ever with me, and all that I have is thine."** He was literally saying, son, you have been faithful. Everything I have you will inherit. Then he went on to imply, *"I thought this was what the church was all about. I thought this was what we were working and praying for—to get your lost brother saved."* **(+)** Read verse 32 with that interpretation in mind. **"It was meet that WE** [you and me] **should make merry, and be glad: for this thy brother was dead,** [Eph. 2:1] **and is alive again; and was lost** [LOST]**, and is found."** This whole chapter is given to inform and charge the saints of God to persevere in the main purpose for their lives, persevere in their efforts to SEEK AFTER SINNERS. The teaching of this chapter is in complete harmony with the practice of Jesus during His personal ministry. His main effort was to reach sinners. Most of the religious crowd did not understand the true purpose of Christianity then and most of the 20th Century church members do not understand it today, but the plain teaching of Jesus... the plain teaching of the Bible... is for the saved to seek after the lost! **(+)**

It is a wise saying, *"THE WISE WIN SOULS."* **"The fruit of the righteous *is* a tree of**

life; and he that winneth souls *is* wise."
PROVERBS 11:30

LESSON FOUR
MONDAY
THE THINGS DONE UNDER

1. The main thought which consumed the mind of Paul was God's _____ _____ _____ for his life.
2. "So that I might finish my _____ with _____."
3. The man's name was _____. The inspired book is the book of _____.
4. Every scientific experiment demands a _____.
5. In his _____ he will give the _____ purpose for man's existence _____ _____ _____.

TUESDAY
THE THING THAT SAVED

1. Jesus spent _____ _____ on the earth_____ leaders.
2. Train the ones won to the _____ where they can win and _____ their own _____.
3. The believer has the _____ _____ of preaching or telling each person in _____ _____ world.
4. If the saved do not go, the sinner will not _____, will not _____ will not call upon _____ _____ _____ _____ _____.
5. The last words of Jesus clearly show that the

saved are to get _____ _____ to
the _____.

WEDNESDAY
THE TESTIMONY OF THE GREATS

1. Then will I teach transgressors thy ways and
_____ shall be _____.
2. "He that _____ souls is _____."

3. I am made all things to all men that I might
by all means _____ _____.
4. Jesus, the Son of God, _____
_____ _____ - _____.
5. As my Father _____ _____
_____ even so send I _____.

THURSDAY
THE TENDENCY OF THE REDEEMED

1. The believers have _____ to discuss
_____ and not _____ as Jesus
commanded.
2. God said He was _____ of their
_____ that he hated them.
3. Jesus strongly _____ the formal
services of the Pharisees and their
_____ of _____.
4. Hast thou _____ the wicked
ones_____ _____?
5. Have you told them _____
_____ _____
_____?

FRIDAY
THE TEACHING OF JESUS

1. It is made up of _____ _____ which shows the _____ for man's life that of _____ _____.

2. Likewise, joy shall be in _____ over one sinner that repenteth.

3. Jesus is clearly illustrated in the _____, _____ and _____ of the sinner by the saved.

4. "I thought this was what we were _____ _____ _____ _____."

5. Most of the _____ _____ did not understand _____ _____ _____ _____ _____ 20th Century church members _____ understand _____ _____.

PERSONAL COMMITMENT

I will strive to submit myself to God's will for my life and strive to win souls to Him personally.

Date: _____

Questions to be asked: My Grade _____

_____
Name

DAILY FAITH BUILDER

LESSON FIVE

GOD'S COMFORTER FOR HIS CHILDREN

Special Thought for the Week

The Holy Spirit was sent by Jesus to lead, protect, empower and comfort us. He is our dearest friend.

Daily Declaration

Since the Holy Spirit is a person and lives within me, I will strive to be conscience of His presence at all times:

CHECK BLOCK AFTER REPEATING

	Mon	Tues	Wed	Thurs	Fri	Sat	Sun
A.M.							
P.M							

Memory Verse

"But ye shall receive power, after that the Holy Ghost is come upon you: and ye shall be witnesses unto me both in Jerusalem, and in all Judea, and in Samaria, and unto the uttermost part of the earth." ACTS 1:8

LESSON FIVE

THE COMFORTER TO HIS CHILDREN

INTRODUCTION: As Jesus faced the dark night before His crucifixion with His disciples, He was keenly aware of their frailties and the human frailty of every believer in the ensuing generations. As the Son of God, housed in human flesh, He could only be in one place at a time. He needed to be with each one of them and have personal fellowship with them in their daily life. He told them, **"...it is expedient** [for your best interest] **for you that I go away: for if I go not away, the COMFORTER will NOT come unto you; but if I depart, I will send him unto you." JOHN 16:7** Jesus was telling the disciples that He would send God, the Holy Spirit who would be with every believer in every situation regardless of where He might be. The word comforter comes from the word, *"paraclyte"* and means *"one standing along side of to aid."* **(+)** It is the same word translated *"advocate"* in John 2:2 when used of Christ. It means *"called to one's aid, appearing on behalf of"*, as a lawyer in a court of law. The thought of helper or strengthener or one who invigorates or makes strong is involved. The word denotes a person who has your best interest at heart and teaches a very close relationship—one along side of to aid—a constant companion.

In this lesson we will study the truths about the believers' Comforter and His work in the world.

MONDAY
I. THE HOLY SPIRIT, A PERSON

A. **HE IS NOT AN INFLUENCE A FLUID, AN ELECTRICAL CURRENT OR A FIGMENT OF ONE'S IMAGINATION.**

He is NOT some vague shadow, He is not someone to blame for one's actions, nor is He an impersonal force; but He is God. **(+)**

B. **THE HOLY SPIRIT IS THE THIRD PERSON OF THE TRININTY FATHER SON AND THE HOLY SPIRIT.**

Jesus commanded the Church to recognize and honor Him at every baptismal service. He said, baptize every convert, **"...in the name of the Father, and of the Son, and of the Holy Ghost:" MATTHEW 28:19** He is equal in every way with the Father and God, the Son. All the divine attributes are ascribed to Him. He is referred to as "He" by Jesus in **JOHN 15:26, "But when the comforter is come... he shall testify of me:"** He has infinite intelligence (I Corinthians 2:11), **(+)** He has a divine will (I Corinthians 12:11), He has feelings (Romans 15:30) and He speaks (I Timothy 4:1).

As Jesus was sent into the world to exalt and reveal the Father, the Holy Spirit was sent to exalt, reveal and glorify the Son. **(+)**

C. **HE IS SENT TO BE A SPECIAL COMFORTER**

The reason the Holy Spirit is called the

Comforter is to stress His primary work in the believer. The title, comforter, (the one along side) denotes the constant presence and help of the Holy Spirit for each believer. He is the believer's constant companion and friend. **(+)** Through the Comforter, Jesus can be with each one of His saints regardless of where he is or what trial he is experiencing. What a wonderful knowledge and strength this should bring to each of God's children.

TUESDAY
II. THE HOLY SPIRIT'S GENERAL WORK

The Holy Spirit has three general areas which He works with mankind. **(+)**

A.   HIS WORK IN RELATION TO CHRIST

In **JOHN 16:13**, Jesus told the disciples that the Holy Spirit, **"...shall not speak of himself..."** The Holy Spirit did not come to promote himself or His own cause. He came to glorify Christ. **"He shall glorify me: for he shall receive of mine, and shall shew *it* unto you." JOHN 16:14(+)** This verse announces the primary work of the Holy Spirit in His relationship toward Christ. He reveals Christ to the world. He helps the believer understand the Bible, so the believer can show the sinner about Christ, the Saviour.

B.   HIS WORK IN RELATION TO THE LOST

"And when he is come, he will reprove [convict] **the world of sin, and of righteousness, and of judgment:" JOHN 16:8** This word *"reprove"* is a strong word which means the Holy Spirit drives the message into the sinner's heart which makes him see how sinful he is in the sight of God. The Holy Spirit reveals the righteousness of Christ and the awfulness of standing in the judgment, lost and undone, without God or hope.

The Holy Spirit strives with sinners (Genesis 6:3) as He did with the Ethiopian Eunuch (Acts 8), Saul of Tarsus (Acts 9) and the household of Cornelius (Acts 10). He strives with the saved to go to the lost. The clear examples of this truth are found in Phillip (Acts 8) and the Apostle Peter (Acts 10). The Holy Spirit's relation to the lost is one of convicting, striving, and working with them as He tries to keep them from going to hell. **(+)** His greatest need is to find a Christian who will be sensitive to Him so He can reach the lost through him.

C.   HIS WORK IN RELATION TO THE SAVED

The Holy Spirit regenerates the believer. (John 3:5, Ephesians 2:1, Titus 3:5, I Peter 1:23) Regenerate means the same as being a born-again believer.

The Holy Spirit comes into the believer and dwells within him at the point of regeneration (I Corinthians 3:16).

The Holy Spirit seals the believer in Christ at the point of conversion unto the rapture (Ephesians 1:13, Ephesians 4:30).

The Holy Spirit is the earnest or guarantee of the inheritance which each believer will receive.

The Holy Spirit helps the believer to put off the "old man" with his filthy deeds (Romans 8:13). **(+)**

The Holy Spirit is the believer's teacher and guide (John 14:18, John 14:26).

The Holy Spirit calls men into special services (Acts 13:2-4).

The Holy Spirit helps the believer in his prayer life (Romans 8:26).

The Holy Spirit works with the believer to produce the fruit of the Spirit in his life (Galatians 5:22-23). ALL of the Christ-like qualities in the believer are produced by the Holy Spirit as the believer yields to His leading.

The Holy Spirit leads the believer to praise the Lord acceptably as He leads to obey the Book of Psalms. **(+)**

WEDNESDAY
III. THE HOLY SPIRIT'S WORK IN THE OLD TESTAMENT

A. HE WORKED IN THE ACT OF CREATION(+)

The first mention of the Holy Spirit in the Old Testament is in **GENESIS 1:2(+)** where it states, **"...the Spirit of God moved upon the face of the** waters." In **GENESIS 1:26**, **"And God said, Let us make man in our image..."** Note that He did not say, *"Let me* [singular] *make man in my image."* He said, **"...Let us** [God the Father, God the Son and God the Holy Spirit] **make man in OUR** [plural] **image..."** God created man as a triune being with a spirit and soul (mind) and body (II Thessalonians 5:23). The psalmist declared, **"By the word of the LORD were the heavens made; and all the host of them by the BREATH of his mouth." PSALM 33:6** and Psalm 104:29-30

B.   HE   SUPERINTENDED   THE   HOLY WRITING (+)

The Holy Spirit is the author of the Bible. The Bible was written by about 40 different writers who were supernaturally directed by the Holy Spirit. Paul boldly declared,

"ALL scripture [referring to the Old Testament as well as the New] *is* **given by inspiration of God, and** *is* **profitable for doctrine, for reproof, for correction, for instruction in righteousness: That the man of God may be perfect, throughly furnished unto all good works."** II TIMOTHY 3:16,17

The word, *"inspiration"*, means *"God-breathed"*. **(+)** Literally, all Scripture is God-breathed or given by the Holy Spirit.

The Apostle Peter adds, **"For the prophecy came not in old time by the will of man: but Holy men of God spake** *as they were* **moved by the**

Holy Ghost." II PETER 1:21. The Bible is verbally inspired and is in truth and is in fact the Word of God. It is an infallible rule of faith and practice. Over 2,000 times in the Old Testament we find the statement, **"Thus saith the Lord."** The Holy Spirit has given us a perfect book in which there is no error or contradiction. The 119th Psalm gives us many things that the Bible does for the believer. Read it carefully for added blessing.

C. HE EMPOWERED SPECIAL MEN FOR SPECIAL SERVICE

The Holy Spirit was not only the moving force in creation and in giving the world the perfect book from heaven which reveals the mind and will of God; but He was the energizing force behind the great prophets and leaders in the Old Testament. **(+)**

God called prophets to preach the Word of God, and those who are well remembered have one thing in common; the Spirit of God came upon them. Note this truth in the following references: Judges 3:10, Judges 6:34, Judges 11:29, Judges 13:24 and Judges 6:34.

When a man became king over God's people, the Spirit of God came upon him. The Spirit of God came upon Saul (I Samuel 11:6). The Spirit of God came upon David (I Samuel 16:13). God anointed and worked with King Solomon in his early reign (II Chronicles 1:1 through II Chronicles 6:42). Many other prophets, such as Elijah were noted for their Spirit-filled preaching. God called Bezaleel and filled him with the Spirit of God so he could direct the building of the tabernacle. Exodus 35:30-31.

In the Book of Joel, the prophet foretells a change in the way God would deal with men. There would come a time, according to Joel, in which God would make available the filling and empowering of the Holy Spirit to all men. In the Old Testament, God only filled and empowered judges, kings, preachers and men called to a special purpose such as Bezaleel. In **JOEL 2:28-32** the Holy Spirit announced a change. Read this prophecy which was fulfilled on the day of Pentecost.

"And it shall come to pass afterward, *that* **I will pour out my spirit upon all flesh; and your sons and your daughters shall prophesy, your old men shall dream dreams, your young men shall see visions: And also upon the servants and upon the handmaids in those days will I pour out my spirit. And I will shew wonders in the heavens and in the earth, blood, and fire, and pillars of smoke. The sun shall be turned into darkness, and the moon into blood, before the great and the terrible day of the Lord come. And it shall come to pass,** *that* **whosoever shall call on the name of the Lord shall be delivered..."**

THURSDAY
IV. THE HOLY SPIRIT'S WORK DURING THE LIFETIME OF THE APOSTLES

Just as the Holy Spirit's ministry was different in the Old Testament, He had a special ministry during the lifetime of the apostles. **(+)** He gave special spiritual gifts to the apostles, plus He used them to write the 27 books of the New Testament. Since the completion of the final word in the Book of Revelation, the Holy Spirit works in a different manner.

A. THE CHURCH UNDER THREE ADMINISTRATIONS

Administrations 1: The Church Was Started By Jesus During His Personal Ministry.

He personally taught and trained them for three and one-half years. In order for you to understand that the Church was started during the ministry of Jesus before the day of Pentecost, consider the following:

The apostles were placed in the Church as officers. "And God hath set some in the church, first apostles..." I CORINTHIANS 12:28 In Luke 6:12-13, after praying all night, Jesus placed the apostles in the Church. It would be impossible to place someone into something which did not exist.

The disciples were taught by Jesus to **"...tell *it* unto the church..." verse 17** (Matthew 18:15-18). Again, it would be difficult if there was no church to tell it to.

The church had a church roll (Acts 1:5) before Pentecost and held an election

(Acts 1:21).

The church was given an age-long commission (Mathew 28-:19-20).

There are several other proofs which clearly teach that the church was first under the direct authority, training and administration of Jesus.

Administrations 2: The Church Was Under the Special Administration of the Holy Spirit During a Limited, Transitional Period. (+)

From the time Jesus ascended into heaven to the time the Bible was completed, the church was under the administration of the Holy Spirit as He worked through the apostles and other chosen workers who possessed special, limited spiritual gifts. In order to clearly understand this special time and how it harmonizes with the Holy Spirit's work in our day, the author will remind the reader of some pertinent facts:

Jesus told the apostles to preach the Gospel to every creature alive on the earth and do it within their lifetime. Mark 16:15, Acts 1:8 and Mathew 28:19-20.

The early churches had no written New Testament to teach, to comfort and to direct them as we have in our churches today.

The early preachers did not have years and years of experience to fall back on and to help them in their decision-making. The apostles had been preaching for only three and one-half years when suddenly they were the world-wide leaders. This feat would be the equivalent of a young man surrendering to preach, spending three and one-half years in Bible College and then assuming the role of college president, president of the national organization, expert in all matters, mature in all judgments and the elder statesman of Christianity—all in a short three and one-half years. To further handicap them, they had no complete Bible and the total world was in open hostility. God had to do something to overcome these insurmountable problems.

In order to offset these tremendous limitations, the Holy Spirit gave special spiritual gifts to these early Christians which were to last until: **(+)**

The Bible was completed

They had evangelized the earth for the first time.

They had lived long enough to establish a natural maturity in the Lord's work in each major land.

Note the spiritual gifts in 1 Corinthians 12:4-10 and I Corinthians 12:28. There are nine separate spiritual gifts listed in I Corinthians 12:8-10. In verse 28, eight more spiritual gifts are listed. Some of these are overlapping.

(1) **The gift of Wisdom** is the gift of using acquired knowledge properly.

(2) **The gift of knowledge.** The Holy Spirit just turns on the light of knowledge in the person's head and he knew it without any effort on his part or previous exposure. Now the believer must study to acquire knowledge. (II Timothy 2:15)

(3)   **Helps-governments-administration.** With thousands of people being saved and added to the church (Acts 2:41-44, 4:4, 5:14, 6:6,7), in a matter of a few days or weeks the Spirit gave some the ability of organization and administration. Now, in our day, it takes years for a person to develop these abilities. Can you visualize a fisherman one day, becoming someone who has to lead, plan, educate and direct tens of thousands of people by the next? In order to make this transition God gave special gifts of helps.

(4) **The gifts of tongues.** This is clearly the gift of languages since they were to preach to every creature which includes the different nationalities of the world. Jesus gave the apostles their field of labor when He said, **"...Jerusalem, and in all Judaea, and in Samaria, and unto the uttermost part of the earth."** ACTS 1:8

On the day of Pentecost the Jewish people who had gathered from at least 17 different countries (Acts 2: 9-11) marveled since they heard the Galilean Jews (disciples) speak **"...in our own tongue, wherein we were born?"** ACTS 2:8 One receives their native tongue at birth.

In that day God would call a man to preach to a certain foreign field and then give him the instant gift to speak in that language. The gift of languages was primarily for the benefit of the unbeliever (I Corinthians 14:22) and was given to the believer so they could communicate the Gospel to them.

These special gifts were for a limited time, until "...**that which is perfect** [complete Word of God] **is come, then that which is in part** [spiritual gifts] **shall be done away.**" I **CORINTHIANS 13:10(+)**

The gift of prophecies shall cease. (I Corinthians 13:8) Why? Because we have the complete, perfect, inspired, 66 books of inspired prophecy.

Tongues shall cease (I Corinthians 13:8) Why? Because the Word has been "...**preached to every creature which is under heaven...**" **COLOSSIANS 1:23** With churches established in every country with people who are national pastors and members. In addition to that practical reason, the spiritual gifts were to serve until the completed Word was given. Then, the church was to pass under the third administration-the Word of God.

(5) **The Holy Spirit's power became** available to every believer. **(+)**The spiritual gifts given to the early disciples were to help them overcome their liabilities and limitations. Spiritual gifts, and the filling or overpowering of the Holy Spirit for soul-winning, witnessing and special services ARE COMPLETELY DIFFERENT AND

SEPARATE FROM EACH OTHER. Spiritual gifts of the Holy Spirit were to serve for a limited time while the empowering spirit for soul-winning and service was to serve for the whole age.

FRIDAY
THE LAST DAYS BEGAN IN DURING THE MINISTRY OF JESUS

When the apostle Peter was asked about what was going on during the day of Pentecost he turned to Joel 2:28-32 to answer their questions. He said, **"...this** [what you see and hear] **is that which was spoken by the prophet Joel;" ACTS 2:16**. Then he quoted those verses. **(+)**

"And it shall come to pass in the last days, saith God, I will pour out of my Spirit upon all flesh: and your sons and your daughters shall prophesy, and your young men shall see visions, and your old men shall dream dreams: And on my servants and on my handmaidens I will pour out in those days of my Spirit; and they shall prophesy: And I will show wonders in heaven above, and signs in the earth beneath; blood, and fire, and vapour of smoke: The sun shall be turned into darkness, and the moon into blood, before that great and notable day of the Lord come: And it shall come to pass, *that* **whosoever shall call on the name of the Lord shall be saved." ACTS 2:17-21**

The last days must have started during Jesus' ministry on earth because Peter said,

"...this is that which was spoken by the prophet Joel; and it shall come to pass in the last days..." If it came to pass in the "last days" then the last days had started back then. **(+)**

Note that old men, young men, servants and scrub women could be filled, not just the select few, such as kings or preachers. Note, the length of the availability of this infilling, *"until the sun be darkened and the moon turned to blood."* This will happen at the close of this age. This simply means that you and I can and should be filled with the Holy Spirit so we can be personal soul-winners. It is for *"all flesh."* **(+)**

Administration 3: The Church Under The Word Of God. When that which is perfect (Holy Bible) was completed, there was no more need for the special gift. They had served their purpose. Now, we all are to mind the same rule. (Phil. 3:16). The rule is the perfect, written Word given by the Holy Spirit. **(+)** Today that perfect Word makes the man of God **"...throughly furnished unto all good works." II TIMOTHY 3:17** There is no further need for special helps or gifts. It is all written down. **(+)** The author, the Holy Spirit, as a special teacher, is available to every believer and will help him understand it.

LESSON FIVE
MONDAY
THE HOLY SPIRIT, A PERSON

1. The word, _____ comes from the word _____ or one called alone or beside of.

2. The Holy Spirit is not an _____ _____. He is _____.

3. He has infinite intelligence _____ _____.

4. The Holy Spirit was sent _____, _____ and _____ God, _____ _____.

5. He is the believer's _____ companion and _____.

TUESDAY
THE HOLY SPIRIT'S GENERAL WORK

1. The Holy Spirit has _____ _____ areas in which He works with _____.

2. He shall _____ _____: for he shall receive of mine and shall _____ it unto you."

3. The Holy Spirit is convicting, striving, and _____ with the _____ in order to keep them from going to _____.

4. The Holy Spirit _____ the believer to "put off the _____ man".

5. The Holy Spirit leads the believer _____ _____ the Lord

acceptably.

WEDNESDAY
THE HOLY SPIRIT WORKED IN
THE OLD TESTAMENT

1. He worked in the _____ _____ _____.

2. The first mention of the Holy Spirit in the _____ Testament is _____.

3. He   Superintended   the   _____ _____.

4. The   word,   _____   means, "_____."

5. The   Holy   Spirit   was   the   _____ _____ behind the great _____ and leaders in the Old Testament.

THURSDAY
THE HOLY SPIRIT'S WORK IN THE LIFE OF
APOSTLES

1. The Holy Spirit had a _____ ministry during the life time of the _____.

2. The church was _____ _____ _____ administration of the Holy Spirit.

3. In order to _____ these tremendous _____ the Holy Spirit gave special _____ gifts.

4. The   special   spiritual   gifts   were   for   a _____ _____.

5. The   Holy   Spirit's   _____   became _____ to every believer.

FRIDAY
THE LAST DAYS STARTED DURING THE MINISTRY OF JESUS

1. He said…_____ (what you_____and_____) is _____ which was spoken by the _____Joel.
2. If it came to _____ in the _____days the _____ days had started back then.
3. This simply means that _____ and _____ can and _____be _____ with the Holy Spirit.
4. The _____is the _____, written word given by the Holy Spirit.
5. There is _____ further need for _____gifts. It _____ all_____down.

PERSONAL COMMITMENT

I will strive to be conscience of the Holy Spirit who lives within me and strive to let Him lead me each day.

Date: _____

Questions to be asked: My Grade _____

_____
Name

DAILY FAITH BUILDER

LESSON SIX

GOD'S CHARGE TO HIS CHILDREN

Special Thought for the Week

The greatest need in our modern churches today is a return to the old fashion practice of being filled and empowered by the Holy Ghost.

Daily Declaration

If I obey the commands of God, I must be filled with His Spirit.

CHECK BLOCK AFTER REPEATING

	Mon	Tues	Wed	Thurs	Fri	Sat	Sun
A.M.							
P.M							

Memory Verse

"And be not drunk with wine, wherein is excess; but be filled with the Spirit;" EPHESIANS 5:18

LESSON SIX

THE CHARGE TO HIS CHILDREN

INTRODUCTION: Jesus gave the Great Commission to the church. It is recorded in the first five books of the New Testament, but in this lesson we want to stress a personal charge to the individual disciple.

MONDAY
I. THE COMMISSION TO THE CHURCH

In order to understand the Great Commission, the accounts found in Matthew, Mark, Luke, John and the Book of Acts must be laid side by side and studied.

A.   A NEGATIVE COMMAND

When we think of the Great Commission we think of the verb, *"go"*. A charge is generally a command to action, but in **LUKE 24:49** Jesus told the disciples to **"...tarry ye in the city of Jerusalem..."** He gave them a negative command.

There was never a time in the history of mankind when sin had shackled and made the world as dark as in the lifetime of Christ. Heresy, paganism and idolatry universally reigned. Everywhere corruption, confusion and death plagued the human race. Jesus had already given the great commission but He WOULDN'T LET THE DISCIPLES GO. **(+)** A few days before, His church had all been scattered. They had fled in fear! They ran home and stayed there behind their locked doors.

Then Christ overcame sin, hell and the grave! He appeared in their midst, and they were transformed! They became grown-up Christians with new courage BUT JESUS WOULDN'T LET THEM GO - HE SAID for them to tarry - to wait. They had been trained. For three and one-half years he had worked with his hand-picked leaders. They had the message that the lost, perishing, masses needed BUT JESUS WOULDN'T LET THEM GO! Their attitude was right, they had the message but they lacked ONE THING. THEY LACKED DIVINE POWER. **(+)** They were to tarry until they were "**...endued with power from on high.**" **LUKE 24:49**

B.   THE POSITIVE COMMAND

As previously stated there are five scriptures which shed light on the complete meaning of the Great Commission. Three of the five accounts of the Great Commission emphasize the need of divine power. Dr. Luke quoted Jesus in **LUKE 24:49, "And, behold, I send the promise of my Father upon you: but tarry ye in the city of Jerusalem, until ye be endued with power from on high."**

In **JOHN 20:22** Jesus "**...breathed on** *them*, **and saith unto them, Receive ye the Holy Ghost:**" **ACTS 1:8** emphatically commanded, **"But ye shall receive power, AFTER that the Holy Ghost is come upon you: and YE SHALL BE WITNESSES...**"**(+)** - The power first; Then, they were to go. The positive command of Jesus in the

Great Commission shows the absolute necessity of divine power if one is to be successful in witnessing.

C. THE NEGATIVE AND POSITIVE COMMANDS

In Ephesians 5:18 we have a negative and positive command all in one verse which denotes the imperative need for a child of God to be filled with the Spirit.

THE NEGATIVE: Don't be drunk with wine. It is sinful and wrong for a child of God to be drunk on liquor. It is a sin.

THE POSITIVE: Be filled with the Spirit. If it is wrong to get drunk, it is wrong for a Christian not to be filled with the Spirit.

Paul said in **verse 17, "Wherefore be ye not unwise, but understanding what the will of the Lord** *is*.**"**

Then he states in **verse 18 "And be not drunk with wine, wherein is excess; BUT BE FILLED WITH THE SPIRIT;"** The will of God is for a child of God to be filled with the Spirit. **(+)**

TUESDAY
II. THE CHAMPIONS WERE ALL FILLED WITH THE HOLY SPIRIT

In the previous lesson we pointed out that the great preachers, kings and judges (means champions) were all filled with the Holy Spirit. In this section we want you to consider the New Testament champions.

A.   JOHN THE BAPTIST

The first outstanding man on the scene was John the Baptist. John was last of the Old Testament prophets and the first New Testament preacher. **(+)**

There is an outstanding rule of Bible interpretation which is called the rule of the first mention. When a new term or doctrine is introduced in the Bible by the Holy Spirit, He always clearly defines the term. Then, as He uses the term later in the Scriptures, He is always true to that definition. This very important rule, the rule of the first mention, applies to John because he is the first New Testament preacher. In our modern Bible colleges and seminaries the stress is on doctrine and social graces. They teach the student public speaking, proper dress, psychology, denominational procedure and proper policy.

John was almost the exact opposite in his dress (a leather girdle, and pants made of a crude, burlap sack material); in his speech (literal bellowing like and ox); in his social graces (lived in the wilderness and ate locust and wild honey); and in his procedure and psychology (call them snakes and vipers, Matthew 3). But in spite of all this, John was highly successful in his ministry. The Bible declared, *"all of Jerusalem, Judea and Samaria"* went out to hear him. In **MATTHEW 11:11** Jesus highly commended John and said concerning him, **"...Among them that are born of women there hath not risen a greater than John..."** Why did

God picture John and place John, the first example of a New Testament preacher, in such a strange environment and life-style? It was done to demonstrate that man should not depend upon his natural and mental attributes, but one must "...**be filled with the Spirit;**" (Ephesians 5:18) in order to become a champion for Christ. John was filled with the Spirit from his mother's womb (Luke 1:15). **(+)** The secret of John's great success...clearly...he was filled with the Holy Spirit.

B.   JESUS, THE SAVIOUR

Jesus was born of the Virgin Mary and lived in the flesh on the earth as the Son of God for 30 years. During this time very little was heard from Him. When the time came for Him to enter into His public ministry, He was baptized by John in the river Jordan and was filled with the Spirit. In **LUKE 4:1** the Scripture states, "**...Jesus being full of the Holy Ghost...**" **(+)** Again in **verse 14** it states that "**...Jesus returned in the power of the Spirit into Galilee...**"

Something began to happen! The Scripture declares in **LUKE 4:14**, "**...there went out a fame of him...**" He went to His synagogue as His custom was and announced that something extraordinary had happened to Him (Luke 4:17-21), He testified that He had entered into His public ministry and "**The Spirit of the Lord** *is* **upon me...**" **(verse 18)**

Peter later described the ministry of Jesus by saying, "**How God anointed Jesus of Nazareth with the Holy Ghost and with power: who went about doing good...**" **ACTS 10:38** Jesus, our great example, told His disciples that because His life and ministry were cut short (only three and one-half years) that those who obeyed Him and followed Him by faith would do greater works and have a greater ministry (John 14:12). There is a reason why this was possible for the disciples to accomplish. Jesus was an example to His disciples and depended upon the help and power of the Holy Spirit for His success in the ministry. Through His example He was manifesting that the secret of ministering is through the divine power of God and not through human wisdom or ability.

C. THE EARLY CHAMPIONS, INCLUDING PASTORS AND DEACONS

The first church turned their world upside down through the power of God and Spirit-filled ministry.

They were told to wait for the promise. (Acts 1:4)

They were told they would have power after the Holy Spirit came upon them. (Acts 1:8)

Peter was filled with the spirit and spoke boldly. (Acts 4:8)

They were filled with the Holy Spirit. (Acts 2:4) and had power and success. (Acts 2:41-42)

The church was filled with the Holy Spirit and spoke the word with boldness. (Acts

4:31)

The early pastors asked the church for seven men (whom I believe were the first deacons) who were *fill of the Holy Spirit.* (Acts 6:-.5)

The first deacon, Stephen, was full of faith and the *Holy Ghost.* (Acts 5)

The new convert, Saul, was filled with the Holy Spirit (Acts 9:17, Acts 13:9) **(+)**

Later, when this new convert had grown into a mighty preacher, he wrote **"And my speech and my preaching *was* not with enticing words of man's wisdom, but in demonstration of the Spirit and of power:"** (I CORINTHIANS 2:4)

Paul, why did you come ministering in the power of God instead of the ability of the flesh? He continued in the next verse by saying, **"That your faith should not stand in the wisdom of men, BUT IN THE POWER OF GOD."** Every champion of God in the entire Bible had the same testimony of success. **(+)** They were used and empowered by the Holy Spirit.

WEDNESDAY
III. THE COMFORTER IS TO FILL THE BELIEVER

A.   IT IS ONE THING TO BE SAVED; IT IS ANOTHER TO BE FILLED.

All believers are indwelt by the Spirit of God,

but all believers are not filled with the Spirit. **(+)** It is one thing to have the Holy Spirit in the Throne Room, that is, in one's heart, but it is entirely a different thing to have the Spirit ON THE THRONE. Many accept Jesus as their Saviour but do not accept Him as their Lord. All believers are not filled with the Spirit or else we would not have the command, **"...be filled with the Spirit." EPHESIANS 5:18.** The first part of that verse states **"And be not drunk with wine, wherein is excess..."** then the command, **"...but be filled with the Spirit;"** On the day of Pentecost the Spirit-filled disciples were accused of being *"full of new wine,"* or drunk. In Acts 2:15-17 Peter corrected the critics by saying, **"For these are not drunken, as ye suppose...But this is that which was spoken by the prophet Joel...I will pour out of my Spirit..."** There is an analogy between being filled with the Spirit and being drunk with wine. **(+)** When one is intoxicated, his whole being is dominated with wine. His talk is different, his walk is different and everything about him is changed. When one is filled with the Spirit, his whole being is dominated from above. One could take a sip of Vodka and no one would know, but if a man drank the whole bottle of Vodka, everyone would know. One can be born of the Spirit and no one would know, but if one was filled with the Spirit then everyone would know about it.

One cannot fill a container which is already full. **(+)** If one is drunk on the things of the world then he will not know anything about being filled with the Spirit.

If he is full of self and what people will think

then he cannot be filled with the Spirit. As pointed out earlier, every believer is indwelled by the Spirit. Often the Holy Spirit is pushed back in some hidden part of the heart.

To be filled with the Spirit means that we bring Him out of the hidden sanctuary and give Him complete control of our whole heart. To be filled is to allow Him absolute control of every single part of our lives. He is to be Lord of our earthen vessel.

B.   THE MAIN REASON FOR THE FILLING OF THE SPIRIT

The Spirit-filled life is one of inward peace and joy. **(+)** The Spirit-filled life is a Spirit-directed life. The Spirit-filled life brings death to self.

The Spirit-filled life is a life of service. The Spirit-filled life is a fruitful life; love, joy, peace, longsuffering, gentleness, goodness, faith, meekness and temperance. The Spirit-filled life brings confidence and boldness.

But the main reason one is to be filled with the Holy Spirit is for witnessing. The main work of the believer is to witness for Christ and to win souls. **(+)** If He is to succeed, he must have divine power. He must be filled with the Spirit.

May God grant each one of us a sincere desire to be filled with the Spirit so we can be used of God and become a blessing to many.

THURSDAY
IV. THE CONDITIONS WHICH PREVENT

THE FILLING

If the Bible clearly teaches that the believer is to witness and win souls and it does; if the Bible teaches that one must be filled with the Spirit in order to be successful in winning souls, and it does; then the question arises, *"Why aren't there more Spirit-filled soul winning Christians today?"* What are the reasons that one who has experienced love and forgiveness of receiving Christ, one who has experienced the thrill of His presence, would reject the will of God, quench the Spirit and choose to go his own way? Why would a believer sacrifice the power and success of a Spirit-filled life in order to go his own way?

Consider the following reasons:

A.   LACK OF A PROPER EXAMPLE BEFORE THEM(+)

New converts do not know how to read their Bibles. They must be taught. From the point of decision to the point where the normal young convert knows how to read and handle God's Word he must depend upon older Christians. During this most impressionable time he learns much more from observing the examples of other Christians than he does from the Bible. As a young, spiritual child he learns as he watches the actions and lifestyles of the older believers. Most of these whom he imitates are not Spirit-filled, soul-winning Christians; therefore, he becomes mislead from the actions of their life and by following their wrong example.

B.   LACK OF KNOWLEDGE OF GOD'S WORD

There is much confusion in the religious world. Perhaps, there is no doctrine which is more thoroughly confused than the doctrine of being filled with the Spirit. There is very little true Bible preaching and teaching on this subject. **(+)** Many pastors, who are good men, are not filled with the Spirit. The same can be stated about Bible College professors, Bible and Sunday school teachers.

If one is not Spirit-filled, if he is not personally winning souls then he will not teach others to win souls or to be filled with the Spirit. **(+)** The average believer, therefore, has no one to clearly teach him about being filled with the Spirit.

C.   LACK OF SEPARATION FROM THE WORLD

God commands, **"Love not the world, neither the things *that are* in the world. If any man love the world, the love of the Father is not in him." I JOHN 2:15. "...know ye not that the friendship of the world is enmity with God? whosoever therefore will be a friend of the world is the enemy of God." JAMES 4:4** A love of material things and a desire to conform to the ways of this world system keeps many believers from being filled with the Holy Spirit. They dress like, talk like, sing like and many times, behave like the lost people of the world. By doing this, they grieve and quench the Holy Spirit. One should constantly be on guard and careful of his Christian deportment.

The very things he sees on television and

hears on the radio (vulgar words in worldly music) grieve the Holy Spirit.

D.   LACK OF SURRENDER TO THE LORD

"...God resisteth the proud, and giveth grace to the humble." I PETER 5:5(+)

Pride hinders a person from fully surrendering to the Lord. What will people think? They will think I am a religious nut, a fanatic. God resisteth the proud, but giveth grace to the humble. Many times a person will become self-sufficient and attempt to do the work of the Lord in his own strength. God resisteth the proud. There are many other things which keep Christians from experiencing the joy and power of a Spirit-filled life.

Love of money, beautiful things, cars, houses

Love of human praise

Selfishness

A Compromising heart

Self-will or stubbornness

Lustful dress or action

Dishonesty and lying

Lack of self-control or anger

All of the above hinder the filling of the Holy Spirit. The Holy Spirit can and will help each believer to have power and victory over each problem in his life. **"… God resisteth the proud, and giveth grace to the humble." I PETER 5:5**

E.   LACK OF TRUST IN GOD

Many Christians are afraid that if they fully and completely surrender their lives to the Lord, He may pull some dirty trick on them. He may send that person through some hardship—if he fully surrenders. Consider the following illustration. I have five children whom I love very dearly. Suppose they came to me and said, *"Dad, we love you and have been thinking of some way that we can really express our love. We have decided to make ourselves completely at your disposal and do anything that you want us to do."* How do you suppose I would respond? Would I request something which would show my love and appreciation; or would I pull some mean dirty trick on them? Would I try to make them miserable or happy?

I would respond by trying to demonstrate my love to them in a greater way than ever before. That is exactly how God responds to His children when they fully surrender to Him. Our heavenly Father stands ready to bless, to enrich, and to fill each of His children if they will only TRUST HIM. **(+)** But lack of faith or trust hinders many from being filled with the Spirit.

FRIDAY
V. THE CONDITIONS WHICH BRING
THE FILLING

May we make it very clear that to be filled with the Spirit does NOT mean that we get more of the Spirit, but that we give him more of ourselves. (+) As we surrender to the Spirit and yield ourselves to Him and are filled with His presence, He is more able to work in and through us, to control us so He may be able to exalt and glorify Christ in and through us.

If the empowerment which comes from the Holy Spirit is so vital...if it is the difference between success and failure...if it is the difference between a believer *"hanging on out of duty"* or having the exciting, happy life which is described as *"joy unspeakable and full of glory"*...if it is that important, then how does one obtain this power? Please consider the following principles:

A. A DESIRE TO HAVE THIS POWER

"...Jesus stood and cried, saying, If any man thirst, let him come unto me, and drink. He that believeth on me, as the scripture hath said, out of his belly shall flow rivers of living water. (But this spake he of the Spirit, which they that believe on him should receive: for the Holy Ghost was not yet *given***; because that Jesus was not yet glorified.)" JOHN 7:37-39 "Blessed** *are* **they which do hunger and thirst after righteousness: for they shall be filled." MATTHEW 5:6** When one is ready to accept the gracious invitation of Jesus, **"...If any man thirst, let him come unto me, and drink..."** he is ready to yield his will to the will and purpose of God. He longs to make a full and complete surrender of himself to the will of God. He is no longer content to have the Holy Spirit as a guest in his house, but he longs to give Him full sway and control of every room.

As one writer stated, you invite Him into the library of your mind, into the dining room of your appetites, into the parlor of your relationships, into the game room of your social life and into the hidden rooms where he has never been allowed before. You give Him the title deed to the whole house and crown Him as your Lord. **(+)** He is Master. You thirst after pleasing Him with an attitude like that one is well on his way to being filled with the Spirit.

B.   AN EMPTINESS OF SELF

One cannot fill a full vessel. It is already full. Many twentieth century Christians walk like the world, talk like the world, dress like the world and live like the world. In doing so, they become enemies of God. (Philippians 3:8, James 4:4) One who is full of the cares of the world grieves the Holy Spirit, and can never hope to be filled with the Spirit. One must come out of the world and be separate, before he can claim the promise in II Corinthians 6:17-18.

Full of Self. Many are so concerned about being notice and receiving the credit that God can't fill them. Others are afraid of what friends or family may think. They are full of self. One must die to self (Romans 6:11) and present their body as a living sacrifice (Romans 12:1) before he can be filled with the Spirit.

C.   AN EARNEST PRAYER FOR POWER

"If ye then, being evil, know how to give good gifts unto your children: how much more shall *your* heavenly Father give the Holy Spirit to them that ask him?" LUKE 11:13

> **A good example:** Jesus said, *"If you parents like to be good to your children by giving them nice presents ..."*

> **How much more**: If you, who are human and naturally selfish like to be nice to your children and give them nice presents, then how much more would your perfect, loving, heavenly Father like to give nice presents to His children?

> **His choice GIFT:** He spared not His Son, but gave Him to suffer and redeem us. How much more will He give us the greatest— best—most prized GIFT; the Gift of being filled, empowered of God...if we will only ASK HIM? **(+)**

> **Jesus promised**: **"Ask, and it shall be given you..." MATTHEW 7:7**

D.   AN OBEDIENCE TO THE SCRIPTURES

As much as one understands, he must obey the teachings of the Bible. Peter answered the questions of the Jewish council in **ACTS 5:29, "...We ought to obey God rather than men."**

After some other remarks, he continues, **"And we are his witnesses of these things; and** *so is* **also the Holy Ghost, whom God hath given to them that obey him."** ACTS 5:32

E.   AN ACCEPTANCE BY FAITH

After one has a desire (thirst) to be filled and empowered by God.

After one has turned from the world and selfish desires.

After he has begun to pray for and ask God to empower him.

After he is striving to obey the Lord and be directed by the Scriptures.

Then, accept God at His word and allow Him to use and fill you. Be willing to be filled. God will not cross your will, but will wait for your surrender. You must be willing to be controlled by Him. When we take our hands off our lives and allow Him full control, then there will be a flood tide of peace and power into our lives. If we hold back the least part, the Spirit's filling will be hindered. Sometimes we are willing to be used of God in some great situation, but do not want to be used in a small place or task. This hinders the Spirit's filling for we have not yielded completely to Him. **"But without faith** *it is* **impossible to please** *him***..."** HEBREWS **11:6 (+)** Do you believe God loves you and wants to use you? Do you believe that He longs to give you the best gift? Do you believe He wants you to obey His command of *"be filled with the Spirit?"*

Do you believe He will fill you if you will allow Him? In Matthew 9:28-29, Jesus asked the blind men if they thought Jesus could heal them. The blind men answered, **"...Yea, Lord."** Jesus then touched their eyes and said, **"...According to your faith be it unto you."** Find a quiet place and go over these principles again.

Remember God gave His Son to die the in-human death of the cross for you. Jesus endured the torments of Hell for you. God gives you your breath and life each day. He allowed you to be born and raised in the land of Bibles and freedom. But your lifetime is brief. This is a short race. He has a will for your life. In order for you to fulfill that will you must have His power. Both you and God cannot be boss in your life. He wants your eyes, ears, lips, hands, feet, mind, heart and will.

He desires to use them to make Himself known unto men.

HOW CAN YOU BE FILLED WITH THE SPIRIT**(+)**

Be cleansed
Be thirsty
Be willing
Be believing
AND

You will be *"filled with the Spirit."*

LESSON SIX

MONDAY
THE COMMISSION TO THE CHURCH

1. Jesus had given the _____ _____ but he _____ let them go.
2. They lacked _____ thing. They lacked _____ _____.
3. You shall receive _____ after the Holy Ghost comes upon you.
4. Don't be drunk with _____ but be filled with the _____.
5. The _____ of God is for a _____ _____ _____ to be filled with the Spirit.

TUESDAY
THE CHAMPIONS WERE FILLED

1. John was the _____ of the Old Testament prophets and the New Testament _____.
2. John was _____ with the Spirit from his mother's womb. Luke 1:15.
3. In Luke 4:1 the Scripture states, Jesus _____ _____ of the Holy Ghost.
4. The new convert, Saul _____ _____ with the Holy Spirit. Acts 9:17, Acts 13:9.
5. Every _____ of God has the same testimony of _____.

WEDNESDAY
THE COMFORTER IS TO FILL

1. All believers _____ _____ with
    the Spirit but all are not _____.
2. There is an _____ between being
    _____ with the Spirit and being
    _____ with wine.
3. One cannot _____ a container which
    is already _____.
4. The Spirit filled life is _____ of inward
    _____ _____ _____.
5. The main work of _____ _____
    is to witness for Christ and _____
    souls.

THURSDAY
THE CONDITIONS WHICH PREVENT

1. Lack of _____ _____ before
    them.
2. There is very little _____ preaching
    and teaching on the _____.
3. If one is not Spirit _____ then he will
    not _____ others to be filled with the
    _____.
4. God resisteth the _____ but giveth
    _____ to the humble.
5. Our Heavenly Father stands ready
    _____ _____ to enrich,
    _____ _____ each of His
    children if they will _____ Him.

FRIDAY
THE CONDITIONS WHICH BRING

1. To be filled with the Spirit does not mean _____ _____ _____ of the Spirit but that _____ _____ Him more of ourselves.
2. You give Him the _____ _____ to your _____ house and crown Him as your Lord.
3. How much more will He give us the _____, _____, most prized gift if we will_____ _____ Him.
4. "Without _____ it is impossible to _____ God."
5. _____ cleansed, _____ thirsty, _____ willing, _____ believing, and you will _____ filled with the Spirit.

PERSONAL COMMITMENT

I will strive to yield myself completely to the Holy Spirit so He can empower me for His Service.

Date: _____

Questions to be asked: My Grade _____

_____

Name

DAILY FAITH BUILDER

LESSON SEVEN

GOD'S COMING FOR HIS CHILDREN

Special Thought for the Week

If the Saints would lift up their eyes and look for His coming, it would lift up their standards and liven up their services.

Daily Declaration

LOOK UP!!! HE MAY COME TODAY!

CHECK BLOCK AFTER REPEATING

	Mon	Tues	Wed	Thurs	Fri	Sat	Sun
A.M.							
P.M							

Memory Verse

"Watch therefore, for ye know neither the day nor the hour wherein the Son of man cometh." MATTHEW 25:13

CHAPTER SEVEN

GOD'S COMING FOR HIS CHILDREN

INTRODUCTION: In the troublesome times just before the seizure, trial and crucifixion of Jesus, He comforted His disciples by telling them of another world. He said, **"Let not your heart be troubled: ye believe in God, believe also in me."** JOHN 14:1

"In my Father's house are many mansions...I go to prepare a place for you. And if I go and prepare a place for you, I WILL COME AGAIN..."JOHN 14:2-3 Since that time, until this present hour, the second coming of Christ has comforted and kept God's children working amidst the troubles and trials of life.

MONDAY
I. THE PROMISE OF HIS COMING

A.   PROMISED BY THE ANCIENTS

From Job, the first book of the Bible written, to the last book, Revelation, the second coming of Christ is the one clear promise held out to mankind. Job asked the question which is on every human heart, **"If a man die, shall he live *again*?"** **(+)**Then he hastened on to answer his own question by saying, **"all the days of my appointed time will I wait, till my change come."** Job 14:14(+)

One scholar states that every one of the 66 books of the Bible clearly states the promise or teaches that Jesus Christ is literally, coming back to this earth bodily. **(+)**

B.   PROMISED BY THE ANGELS

The most forceful promise by the angelic host is found in **ACTS 1:11. (+)** **"...Ye men of Galilee, why stand ye gazing up into heaven? This same Jesus, which is taken up from you into heaven, shall so come in like manner as ye have seen him go into heaven."**

C.   PROMISED BY THE APOSTLES

The first New Testament book written was the book of First Thessalonians and its theme - The Personal, imminent return of Jesus to the earth. There are five chapters in that book and each chapter closes with a reference to His coming.

John, the beloved disciple, completes the inspired writings in the book of Revelation by saying, **"...Even so, come, Lord Jesus."** **REVELATION 22:20** Every New Testament book and every doctrine of the church has reference to the second coming.

It is one of the two most referred-to doctrines in the Bible.

D.   PROMISED BY THE ALMIGHTY

Jesus promised, **"...I will come again..."** **JOHN 14:3** In fact, the last promise in the Bible is the simple reassuring statement by Jesus, **"...Surely I come quickly..."(+)** REVELATION

22:20 The clearest promises in the word of God have to do with the literal second coming of Christ for His children.

TUESDAY
II. THE PROCEDURE OF HIS COMING

In referring to the resurrection, Paul said, **"...every man in his OWN ORDER..." I CORINTHIANS 15:23(+)** God has a procedure, or order, in the resurrection.

A. TWO RESURRECTIONS

In **REVELATION 20:6**, John said, **"Blessed and holy *is* he that hath part in the first resurrection..."** The first resurrection is composed of the saved and proceeds the second resurrection of the lost by 1,000 years (Revelation 20:1-15).

The first resurrection is followed by the judgment seat of Christ in which only the saved will appear. The faithful saints will rule and reign on this earth with Christ for 1,000 years. This is called The Millennium. The devil is chained in Hell and the world will enjoy complete peace. At the end of The Millennial reign, the lost (their spirits) will be brought up out of Hell while their bodies will be resurrected from the earth. Their spirits and bodies will be reunited and they will stand in judgment before the Great White Throne Judgment. Jesus spoke of these future resurrections and judgments in **JOHN 5:27-29. (+)**

"And hath given him authority to execute judgment also...in the which all that are in the

graves shall hear his voice, And shall come forth; they that have done good, unto the resurrection of life; and they that have done evil, unto the resurrection of damnation."

B.   TWO PHASES OF HIS COMING

The first coming of Jesus to the earth, as a man, spanned over a 33 ½ year period. We refer to His birth, life and death as one coming even though it covered His complete lifetime.

Jesus is coming back to this earth a second time. He will come as a thief for His saints and catch them out of the world. Seven years later, He will come to this earth as a conquering King with His saints.

Paul told the saints in Thessalonica that Jesus would come "...as a thief in the night." I THESSALONIANS 5:2 In I Thessalonians 4:17, Paul instructs them that the saved will meet Jesus in the air.

In verse 14-15 of the Book of Jude, it talks about the time Jesus will come to stand on the earth. It states that "...the Lord cometh with ten thousands of his saints, To execute judgment upon all..." Zechariah, the prophet, tells of His coming back to the earth and standing on the Mount of Olives (Zechariah 14:1-4).

We have one coming, with two distinct phases. (+)

He comes at the beginning of what scholars call the tribulation period. This period is seven years in length.

At the first of this period He comes and His saints rise from the earth and meet Him in the air. They enter into a time of rejoicing and victory which takes place in heaven.

At the end of the tribulation, He comes back to the earth with His saints, stops the Battle of Armageddon, puts the devil down in Hell, judges the nations and goes into the 1,000 year millennial reign.

C. TWO CHANGES DURING HIS COMING

These changes will take place faster than a human tongue can describe them. In heaven we have the spirits of the saints which have died in the Lord.

Their bodies are sleeping in the earth. When Jesus comes to resurrect their bodies from the dead, He will bring the saints who are in heaven with Him.

"For if we believe that Jesus died and rose again, even so them [their bodies] **also which sleep** [in the grave] **in Jesus will God bring** [He is coming from heaven] **with him. I THESSALONIANS 4:14**

We, the saved, will be living in our old human bodies and suddenly the Lord will come. **"Behold, I shew you a mystery; We shall not all sleep** [die], but we shall all be changed, In a moment, in the twinkling of an eye, at the last trump: for the trumpet shall sound, and the dead shall be raised [resurrected] incorruptible, and we shall be changed." I CORINTHIANS 15:51-52 Paul speaks of this change in PHILIPPIANS 3:21. He said, "Who shall change our vile body, that it may be fashioned like unto his glorious body..." In I THESSALONIANS 4:16-17, Paul describes the two changes, "...THE DEAD IN CHRIST shall rise first: THEN WE WHICH ARE ALIVE AND REMAIN shall be caught up together with them in the clouds, to meet the Lord in the air..." This change in our bodies is called the Rapture of the Saints and takes place at the first resurrection. (+)

D. TWO SEPARATIONS AT HIS COMING

"Then shall two be in the field; the one [saved] shall be taken, and the other [lost] left. Two women shall be grinding at the mill; the one [saved] shall be taken, and the other [lost] left. Watch, therefore: for ye know not what hour your Lord doth come." MATTHEW 24:40-42 The saved will be caught away while the lost shall be left behind. Jesus could come today! If He came today would all your family be taken? Wives will leave lost husbands while parents will leave their children behind. Dads will awake to an empty house, their saved family caught away in the rapture. (+) This eternal separation will take place at His coming. It behoves Christians to live right, pray and get their household saved.

WEDNESDAY
III. THE POINT OF HIS COMING

A. SUDDENLY...IN THE SKY

The night was dark. Overhead was a cloud. Suddenly, a flash of lightning lit up the whole countryside! It startled me! **Matthew 24:27** popped into my mind! **"For as the lightning cometh out of the east, and shineth even unto the west; so SHALL also the coming of the Son of man be."** That's exactly how it will happen one of these days. Jesus will come back unexpectedly, and suddenly, like a flash of lightning, He will be back! **(+)**

Jesus illustrated his unexpected, sudden coming by referring to the people who lived in Noah's day who were caught by surprise. In **MATTHEW 24:38** He said, **"...they were eating and drinking, marrying and giving in marriage..."** and bang! The flood caught them unprepared and swept them all away. In **verse 36** He said, **"But of that day** [his coming] **and hour knoweth no** *man*, **no, not the angels of heaven, but my Father only."** In **verse 42** He warns, **"Watch therefore: for ye know not what hour your Lord doth come."** Don't be like the people of Noah's generation caught unprepared by the sudden judgment even though they had been warned of its coming. You may take one step on solid ground, but your next step will be in the air as you join the millions of saints who will meet Jesus in the air. **(+) "And what I say unto you I say unto all, WATCH." MARK 13:37**

B. SECRETLY - AS A THIEF

"...the day of the Lord so cometh as a thief in the night." I THESSALONIANS 5:2

A thief doesn't send clues ahead for the householder to know when he's going to break in and steal. The thief slips in undetected, steals the prize possessions and then slips out. **"...the Lord so cometh as a thief in the night."**

People like to study the Bible and find out all about this precious doctrine of the Lord's return. Many have gone far beyond prophecy as they talk about the signs of His coming. Everything to them is a sign. Perhaps this is the reason that some people are skeptical and do not believe this doctrine. He is coming; we know that. But we do not know when He is coming. **(+)** The angels don't know. It is something which only God knows. Dr. Luke put it, **"...the Son of man cometh at an hour when ye think not."** LUKE 12:40 McCheyne, a famous, Scottish preacher once asked a congregation, *"Do you think Christ will come tonight?"* One after another of them answered, *"I think not."* When they had finished answering, the great preacher quoted, **"... the Son of man cometh at an hour when ye think not."**

D. L. Moody gives the following comment from C. H. Spurgeon on the text, **"...It is not for you to know the times or the seasons, which the Father hath put in his own power."** ACTS 1:7 Spurgeon said, *"If I were introduced into a room where large numbers of parcels were stored up, and I was told there was something good for me, I* *should begin to look for that which had my name upon it, and when I come upon a parcel and saw in pretty big letters, 'IT IS NOT FOR YOU', I should leave it alone.* **(+)** *Here, here, is a casket of knowledge marked, '*...IT IS NOT FOR YOU TO KNOW THE TIMES OR THE SEASONS, WHICH THE FATHER HATH PUT IN HIS OWN POWER.'"

Cease to meddle in matters which are concealed, and be satisfied to know the things which are clearly revealed. If Christ had said, *"I will NOT come back for 2,000 years"*, none of His disciples would have begun to watch for Him until the time was near, but we are to always be looking for His coming. So God does not tell us when Jesus may come, but He commands us, *"to watch."* Just as Simeon and Anna watched for His first coming we are to watch for His second coming.

C.   SELECTIVELY - FOR HIS SAINTS

Someone said Jesus isn't coming just for the Baptists. He isn't coming just for the Methodists or the Pentecostals. He is coming just for His own. There is no general judgment in which all the dead, both the saved and the lost, will be judged. This is basically what many in the world believe. They think that He will come and if they have been good enough; that is, their morality and right deeds outweigh their doings and sins, they will go to heaven. If not, then they will go to hell. This belief is completely unscriptural and false. Jesus will come back as a thief. Suddenly and without warning, those who have confessed their sins to God and have been born again will be caught up to meet the Lord in the air. The others, even though by our human standards may be good neighbors and considered good citizens and people, will be left behind. It is expedient that we lead our friends and neighbors to salvation. **(+)** The angel may have the trumpet to his lips even now - preparing to sound!

THURSDAY
IV. THE PURPOSE OF HIS COMING

There are at least three purposes which God wants to accomplish by His coming for His saints. There are many other reasons for His coming back to the earth which we will study in a future lesson.

A.   LIFT THEIR MIND

The Bible is full of admonishments to the child of God to be separated from the world. **"Love not the world, neither the things** *that are* **in the world..." I JOHN 2:15 "And be not conformed to this world: but be ye transformed..." ROMANS 12:2 "Lay not up for yourselves treasures upon earth..." MATTHEW 6:19** On and on it goes, but these commands seem to fall on deaf ears. The major thing which kills the working of the Holy Spirit and hinders the effectiveness of the Lord's people is their worldliness. The doctrine of the imminent return of Jesus Christ was given to correct that situation and cause the saints to live a clean, spiritual life. The command is clearly stated in **COLOSSIANS 3:1-4. "If ye then be risen with Christ, seek those things which are above...Set your affection on things above...when Christ...shall appear...then shall ye also appear with him in glory." "Beloved, now are we the sons of God, and it doth not yet appear what we** shall be: but we know that, when he shall appear, we shall be like him; for we shall see him as he is. **And every man that hath this hope in him PURIFIETH HIMSELF, even as he is pure."** I JOHN 3:2-3 If a child of God really believes in the imminent return of Jesus Christ it lifts his mind off of the world and causes him to live a clean life. **(+)**

B.   LIVENS HIS HOPE

A child of God can smile and walk with an uplifted head in the darkest hours of life, because of the blessed hope, the hope of His return. Death does not end it all. There is a better day ahead. We will rule and reign with Christ for 1,000 years **(+)** **"...I will come again, and receive you unto myself; that where I am, *there* ye may be also."** John 14:3 **"Looking for that blessed hope, and the glorious appearing of the great God and our Saviour Jesus Christ;"** TITUS 2:13 A firm conviction of the coming Saviour lifts and livens one's hope, even in the darkest, most troublesome times.

C.   LINES HIS POCKETS

When I use the expression, *"lines his pockets"*, the author is trying to vividly illustrate that the Lord is going to reward His people for their faithful, God-like living. **(+)** God will show the world that it paid to serve Jesus.

"And, behold, I come quickly; and my reward *is* with me, to give every man according as his work shall be." REVELATION 22:12 God saved man for a purpose (II Timothy 1:9), and gave him a path to walk in (Ephesians 2:10). He commanded his people to occupy (Luke 19:11-13) or work until He returns. Some will be obedient and work until He returns. Some will be obedient and be rewarded, while others will not be looking for His return and will suffer great loss. **"...he himself shall be saved; yet so as by fire." (+) I CORINTHIANS 3:15** *God motivates His children to live for Him by offering great and eternal rewards. One day those rewards will be laid at the feet of Jesus, but God promises to reward every child if he walks lawfully. (II Timothy 2:5 - II Timothy 2:12)*

This life will soon be past,

Only what's done for Jesus will last... **(+)**

FRIDAY
V. THE POWER OF HIS COMING

There is something more certain than death and taxes; **(+)** the second coming of Christ. Jesus may come before you pay your next taxes. He could come today.

The great demonstration of power will take place when Jesus comes back to the earth with His saints at the end of the tribulation. At that time, Jesus will stop the Battle of Armageddon, judge the nations, bind and cast the devil into hell and other notable facts of strength. We would like to consider the power which transforms men's lives when they have a clear awareness of the imminent coming of Jesus for His saints.

A. THE POWER TO GET YOUR HOUSE SECURED

In the midst of warning people that they didn't know when the Son of man would return and that His return would separate family members (Matt. 24:39-44), Jesus makes this comment, **"But know this, that if the goodman of the house had known in what watch the thief would come, he would have watched, and would not have suffered** [allowed] **his house to be broken up."** (**vs. 43**) **(+)** The application is, if the saved would have known when the Son of God was coming he would have gotten all of his family saved-and his family circle would not have been broken by some going in the rapture while others are left behind. The saints in Thessalonica endured tremendous afflictions in order to win their countrymen. The principle which motivated them to endure the tribulation and to live in such urgency was, they were waiting and looking for Christ's coming (I Thessalonians 1:6-10). When people vividly believe that Christ could come before the night ends it causes them to secure the household by weeping, witnessing and winning them to the Lord.

B. THE POWER TO GET YOUR ACCOUNTS SETTLED.

A member wouldn't go to bed Sunday night with his Lord's tithe in his pocket if he believed Jesus was coming on Monday morning. **(+)**

A deacon wouldn't have ought against his brother if he truly believed Jesus was coming before sundown.

Un-confessed sin would be confessed.

Wrongs would be made right.

There would be no beer in the ice box and the unchristian apparel would all go into the trash.

The junk music would go, along with the ungodly books.

The power of His coming would put gentleness, love and faithfulness back in the forefront - **"And every man that hath this hope** [vivid awareness of His coming] **PURIFIETH HIMSELF, EVEN AS HE IS PURE." I JOHN 3:3 (+)**

C. THE POWER TO GET YOUR PULSE STARTED.

Many of God's people manifest the attitude, *"If we don't get around to it today there is always tomorrow."* This slothful, lukewarm attitude produces a careless, indifferent atmosphere which makes God sick. Jesus told the church of the Laodiceans to **"...be zealous therefore, and repent." REVELATION 3:19**

Paul told the Romans not to be **"...slothful in business..."** but **"...fervent** [boiling] **in spirit; serving the Lord;" ROMANS 12:11(+)** The fervent preaching of the coming of the Son of God causes a fervent spirit in the saints. The very reason God left the actual time of His Son's second coming in doubt and commanded the church to **"Watch therefore: for you know not what hour your Lord doth** come." **MATTHEW 24:42** was to produce zeal and alertness in His children. He gave them their jobs according to their abilities and told them to get their work done. If He came back and they did not have their work done due to unfaithfulness or slothfulness they would be beaten with many stripes. If they worked then He would reward them. This commandment and exhortation is found in Luke 12:35-48. Jesus gave the punch line in **verse 40** when He said, **"Be ye therefore ready also: for the Son of man cometh at an hour when you think not."**

Have you gotten your work done?

Is your family saved?

Are you working as if Jesus may come at any moment?

If He came back now, would you hear His *"well done"*....or would He say, *"Throw that wicked and slothful servant into outer darkness?"* The very thought of the truthfulness concerning the second coming of Christ GETS ONE'S PULSE STARTED.

LOOK UP, BROTHER!
HE MAY COME TODAY!!

LESSON SEVEN

MONDAY
THE PROMISE OF HIS COMING

1. Job asked the question which is on _____ _____ _____, "if a man _____ shall he live again?"
2. _____ the days of my appointed _____ will I _____ till my change come."
3. One scholar states that _____ of the_____ _____ states the promise or teaches the literal, bodily coming of Christ.
4. The most forceful _____ by the angelic host is found in _____ _____.
5. "Surely _____ come quickly."

TUESDAY
THE PROCEDURE OF HIS COMING

1. Paul said, "every man in _____ _____ _____" I Corinthians 15:23
2. Jesus spake of these _____ _____ in John 5:28-29.
3. We have _____ coming with _____ distinct phases.
4. The changes of our bodies is called the _____ of the _____
5. Dads will awake to an _____ _____, their saved family _____ _____ in the rapture.

WEDNESDAY
THE POINT OF HIS COMING

1. Jesus will come back _____ and _____ like a _____ of lightning.
2. You may take _____ _____ on solid _____ but your _____ step may be in the _____.
3. He is coming; we _____ that; but we do not know _____ he is coming
4. It _____ _____ for you. I should _____ it alone.
5. It is _____ that we lead our friends and neighbors _____ _____.

THURSDAY
THE PURPOSE OF HIS COMING

1. If a child of God really believes in _____ _____ return of Christ it _____ his mind _____ the world and causes him to _____ a clean life.
2. We will _____ and reign with Christ for _____ years.
3. The author is trying to _____ illustrate that the _____ is going to _____ his people.
4. "He shall be _____; yet _____ _____ by fire." I Corinthians 3:15
5. This life will _____ be past, only what's done for Jesus will _____.

FRIDAY
THE POWER OF HIS COMING

1. There is something _____ _____ than _____ and _____.

2. "He _____ _____ watched, and _____ _____ _____ suffered _____ his house to be broken up".

3. A member wouldn't go to bed _____ _____ with _____ _____ _____ in his pocket if he believed that Jesus was coming on _____ _____.

4. Every man that hath this hope _____ _____ of his coming _____ _____.

5. But fervent _____ in spirit, _____ _____ _____.

PERSONAL COMMITMENT

I will do everything in my power to be more mindful of the imminent return of Christ.

Date: _____

Questions to be asked: My Grade _____

_____

Name

DAILY FAITH BUILDER

LESSON EIGHT

GOD'S CROWNS FOR HIS CHILDREN

Special Thought for the Week

The crowns you wear in the next age will depend upon the cross you share in this age.

Daily Declaration

God offers me these tremendous crowns in order to inspire me to do my best for Him on a day by day basis so He can reward me eternally.

CHECK BLOCK AFTER REPEATING

	Mon	Tues	Wed	Thurs	Fri	Sat	Sun
A.M.							
P.M							

Memory Verse

"Look to yourselves, that we lose not those things which we have wrought, but that we receive a full reward." II JOHN 8

LESSON EIGHT

THE CROWNS FOR HIS CHILDREN

INTRODUCTION: In order to capture His children's attention and cause them to give themselves completely to the work of God, crowns are offered to them for faithful, dedicated service. In this lesson we will study the subject of crowns or rewards.

MONDAY
I. REWARDS OFFERED AFTER SALVATION

A.   ETERNAL LIFE IS A FREE GIFT

"...the gift of God is eternal life through Jesus Christ our Lord." ROMANS 6:23 (+) That's right, the Word of God declares that eternal life is a free gift. Eternal life in heaven is the greatest gift a person could ever receive; and God said it is a gift which is absolutely free.

How long does it take to receive a gift? A gift is offered to you; you reach out and take it, and it is yours. You do not have to pay for a gift. All a person has to do is receive it and it is his.

B.   ETERNAL LIFE IS TO BE RECEIVED

How does one receive eternal life? He receives the gift of eternal life when he takes Jesus Christ as his personal Saviour. Eternal life is in a person. When he receives Him, he receives eternal life.**(+)**

"And this is the record, that God hath given to us eternal life, and this life is in his Son. He that hath the Son hath life..." I JOHN 5:11-12

Keep this fact in mind, eternal life is in a person and when you receive that person (Christ) as your personal Saviour then you have eternal life. In **I JOHN 5:13, it states, "...that ye may KNOW that ye have eternal life..."** Eternal life is a present tense possession. A person can be as assured of his salvation as one knows that he is married. A mother knows that she is the mother of three children; she can have the same assurance of her salvation. Eternal life is a gift which one enjoys now, but rewards must be earned and are given out at a future date.

C. ETERNAL LIFE IS DIFFERENT FROM REWARDS

Many try and make eternal life a reward for faithful service. No, eternal life is a free gift one obtains when he receives Jesus Christ as his personal Saviour. It is received in this life and one can know that he now possesses it. Paul states that rewards will be given according to the way the individual works and lives for God. **"...every man shall receive his own reward according to his own labour." I CORINTHIANS 3:8 (+)**

It will help one to understand salvation and rewards if he sees that there are three great differences between the two.

Salvation is a free gift while a reward must be earned. (+)

A child of God has eternal life now, while rewards must be earned and will be given out at the judgment seat of Christ. **(+)**

The personal salvation of the sinner always referred to the past tense, SAVED: while the giving of rewards is in the future at His coming (Revelation 22:12).

TUESDAY
II. REWARDS OFFERED FOR MOTIVATION

A.   KIDS IN SCHOOL

Many parents worry with, fuss at and threaten their kids constantly as they strive to obtain their co-operation in doing their homework. When this fails they complain, feel like a failure and place the child on restrictions. They talk to the child until they are *"blue in the face"* but it doesn't seem to penetrate. They struggle with the child as he makes slow progress in his education. **(+)** Other parents *"throw up their hands"* in frustration and give up.

B.   KIDS MAKE LIMITED PROGRESS UNTIL THEY ARE MOTIVATED (+)

Then something happens! The kid is transformed. He has new interest in his grades. He takes the initiative in doing his homework and begins to make remarkable progress. His attitude toward life takes a definite upswing and he suddenly comes alive. The parents do not have to stand over him any more.

What happened?

As a salesman might say, *"Something hit his hot button"*, or interest center. **(+)** Something or someone has gotten his attention and is motivating him.

It may be he wants to make the honor roll or dean's list. He may want the *"five dollars"* which dad promised for every "A" on his report card. He may have gotten a keen feeling of self-gratification it well enough to do it again. He may have wanted to make the team, or that certain *"one"* caught his eye and so he begins to take pride in order to impress them. Something came along which motivated him to apply himself.

C. GOD'S KIDS IN SCHOOL

Many pastors worry with, fuss at and threaten their members constantly as they strive to obtain their cooperation in living for the Lord. When this doesn't secure proper growth in the Lord's work, the pastor feels like a failure and preaches until he is *"blue in the face"*, but it seems very little of his preaching penetrates.

Some pastors join in the chorus of the *"last day blues."*

Others throw up their hands in frustration and all but say, *"What's the use?"*

D. MEMBERS MAKE LIMITED PROGRESS UNTIL THEY ARE MOTIVATED (+)

Just as parents try to show their kids that studying, doing homework and giving their best in the classroom is good for *"the kid,"* so do the pastors try to impress in their members that it is for *"their good."*

There must be something which will hit the members *"hot button,"* catch his attention and secure his full dedication in the Lord's work. There must be something which will cause his attitude to take a definite upswing and cause him to come alive in the Lord's work. The pastor would not have to stand over him anymore; there must be something to give the member new initiative and dedication. THERE IS! **(+)**

WEDNESDAY
III. REWARDS OFFERED TO PROPEL
ETERNAL GLORY

A.   LOOK LIKE HIM

"...we know that, when he shall appear, we shall be like him..." I JOHN 3:2 (+) "Who shall change our vile body, that it may be fashioned like unto his glorious body..." PHILIPPIANS 3:21

One could touch and feel it. (John 20:27)

He ate food. (Luke 24:42)

He disappeared and was at another place in an instant. (Luke 24:31)

He materialized through the wall. (John 20:19)

Our new body will not be flesh and blood (I Corinthians 15:50-51). It will be *"flesh and bone"* (Luke 24:39). It is incorruptible (v. 42); no decay, sickness or pain. It is glorious (v. 43). Compare the transfiguration. Some believe it will be like the bodies of Adam and Eve's before the fall. It is powerful (v.43); not tired or weak. It is spiritual. In this life the soul is the life of the body, but there the spirit will be the life of the body. It is heavenly (v. 47-49).

The believer's new eternal body will be incorruptible, full of glory, powerful and a spiritual body. (I Cor. 15:42-44). But best of all - we will have a body like unto Jesus and will look like Him!

B.   LIVE LIKE HIM

In the 1,000 year reign on this earth Jesus will rule as King of Kings and Lord of Lords.

Some believers will reign with Him for 1,000 years (Rev. 20:6). **(+)**

Some of God's children will be heirs of God and joint heirs with Jesus Christ (Romans 8:17).

Some of God's children will be promoted and be over 10 cities (Luke 19:11-27).

Some will share with Jesus on His throne (Revelation 3:21).

Some will shine in the brightness of the

firmament as stars forever and ever (Daniel 12:3).
Some will be partakers of His eternal glory (I Peter 5:1).

Some will receive a hundredfold on their investment (Matthew 19:29).

Hallelujah! Jesus is THE King. He is going to reign as a King. He is going to live like a King, and some are going to live like Him. **(+)**

C.   LEARN LIKE HIM

Jesus was the eternal Son of God, but when He came to the earth He lived like a man, so He would become an example to the believer.

"Though he were a SON [Son of God], yet learned he obedience by the things which he suffered;" HEBREWS 5:8

"Let this mind be in you, which was also in Christ Jesus: Who, being in the form of God, thought it not robbery to be equal with God: But made himself of no reputation, and took upon him the form of a servant, and was made in the likeness of men: And being found in fashion as a man, he humbled himself, and became obedient unto death, even the death of the cross." PHILIPPIANS 2:5-8

Before we get to the punch line in verses nine through eleven, consider what Paul said in these verses:

Have the mind of Jesus.

Jesus made Himself of no reputation.

Jesus became a servant.

Jesus was obedient to God's will - to die on the cross.

Now note the results of the humble Son of God's obedience to God's will and desire; **"Wherefore God also hath highly exalted him, and given him a name which is above every name: That at the name of Jesus every knee should bow, of** *things* **in heaven, and** *things* **in earth, and** *things* **under the earth; And** *that* **every tongue should confess that Jesus Christ** *is* **Lord, to the glory of God the Father."** (verse 9-11)

The believer needs to learn:

Suffer awhile and become a mature, established, strong and settled Christian (I Peter 5:10).

Tribulations bring patience and steadfastness (Romans 5:5). **(+)**

All things are designed by God for our good (Romans 8:28).

Light afflictions bring eternal glory (II Corinthians 4:17).

If one suffers with Him he will reign with Him (II Timothy 2:12).

Jesus said He came not to be ministered to but to minister. He said, **"...whosoever will be great among you** [the children of God]**, let him be your minister; And whosoever will be chief among you, let him be your servant:" MATTHEW 20:26-27**

Among the names on God's great honor roll of names is a place for your name if you learn like Jesus, to MAKE OF YOURSELF NO REPUTATION, HUMBLE YOURSELF, AND GIVE YOUR LIFE AWAY IN HIS SERVICE. **(+)**

THURSDAY
IV. REWARDS OFFERED AS CROWNS

The rewards which will be bestowed at the judgment seat of Christ are called crowns. Crowns are symbolic of royalty and speak of the positions which those who win the crowns will have - ruling and reigning with Christ for 1,000 years.

The term "judgment seat of Christ" comes from the Greek, BEMA and does not carry the thought of a court room scene or a tribunal such as was held at the close of World War II for the Nazi war criminals. But the term BEMA, translated, *"judgment seat"*, is like the old Olympic Games, in which the former champions set up on the Bema stand at the end of the race and cheered the contestants on. The Christian heroes are the heroes of faith found in Hebrews 11.

These past champions were great achievers

for Christ. Through faith and often times at the expense of great suffering they ran their race on this earth and fulfilled their purpose. They earned the approval of God and are sitting as "witnesses" cheering for the saints who are now running their race. Jesus is the chief champion on the Bema stand. Read Hebrews 11:1-40 and Hebrews 12:1-4 with these thoughts in mind.

"Wherefore seeing we also are COMPASSED ABOUT WITH SO GREAT A CLOUD OF WITNESSES, let us lay aside every weight, and the sin which doth so easily beset *us*, and let us run with patience the race that is set before us, LOOKING UNTO JESUS THE AUTHOR and finisher of *our* faith; who for the joy that was set before him endured the cross, despising the shame, and is set down at the right hand of the throne of God." HEBREWS 12:1-2

There are five major crowns offered to the saints. We will identify them and give a brief description of why they are offered.

A.   THE CROWN OF REJOICING

The crown for soul-winning

This is the first crown mentioned in the New Testament since the book in which it is found was the first of the New Testament books written. Soul winning is the primary work of the believer. **"For what *is* our hope, or joy, or CROWN OF REJOICING?** *Are* **not even ye** [the ones Paul had won] **in the presence of our Lord Jesus Christ at** his coming?" I **THESSALONIANS 2:19** "Therefore, my brethren [ones he had won in Philippi] dearly beloved and longed for, my joy and crown..." PHILIPPIANS 4:1

Tendency or danger

The people of God have a tendency to be distracted by the beauty and pleasure of this world. They are distracted by:

- **a desire to become a star on a team**
- **a desire to be the best on the job**
- **a desire to win a promotion**
- **a desire to be seen**
- **a desire to earn a reward or recognition**

The world offers a good time. People want to be happy. They are looking to have fun.

The danger to the child of God is being distracted from his main purpose of soul-winning.

The purpose for which this eternal crown is offered

The name, crown of rejoicing, denotes the effect of winning someone - there is joy! **(+) "They that sow in tears shall reap in joy." PSALM 126:5** There is rejoicing on earth, **"...come again with rejoicing..." PSALM 126:6** Joy in heaven (Luke 15:10). Joy to the sinner - but soul-winning is not just fun now, its joy will never end. It will produce greater joy, as we stand with those we won, **"...at his coming?" I THESSALONIANS 2:19** What an eternal joy it will be to see a great host of souls walking the streets of glory, brought to the knowledge of salvation as a result of one's efforts for Him. Everyday as we meet them their smile will bring constant joy to our hearts. No wonder He named the first crown, the soul-winners crown, THE CROWN OF REJOICING.

B.   THE CROWN INCORRUPTIBLE

The Crown Incorruptible is called the "Victor" Crown. (+) It is given to those who do not yield to the fleshly pleasures of this world, who do not allow themselves to be diverted from the Master's work by worldly amusement and involvement. This crown is given for right living. The child of God will not win many people to Christ if he doesn't live right. So the next crown is called the Incorruptible Crown. The context of these verses shows that Paul is talking about service and rewards.

"Know ye NOT that they which run in a race run all, but one receiveth the prize? So run, that ye may obtain. And every man that striveth for mastery is temperate in all things. Now they *do it* to obtain a corruptible crown; but we AN INCORRUPTIBLE." I CORINTHIANS 9:24-25

The tendency or danger of the saved

Man has a tendency of wanting to be accepted, of conforming, of keeping up with the latest fashions. God commands His people to be separated from the world. In his talk, walk, dress and manners the believer has a tendency to compromise Bible standards.

The purpose for offering this Incorruptible Crown

In offering this reward God is stressing His standard of acceptable Christian conduct. God stated that my ways are not your ways – **"For *as* the heavens are higher than the earth, so are my ways higher than your ways..."** ISAIAH 55:9 Many Christians can't see any harm in the music they listen to, some of the television they watch, their dress standard, the length of the man's hair which manifests a compromising spirit. It is not long like the world but neither is it short like the dedicated, soul-winning, Christian leadership. It is in between; a compromise.

God offers an eternal crown for those who take an open stand as a Christian, who act like, dress like, talk like and live like a disciple (an imitator of Christ).

Jesus asked, "Do you want to rule with me for 1,000 years? Then live a clean, disciplined, Christian life and I will award you the incorruptible Crown at the Judgment Seat."

C.   THE CROWN OF LIFE

This is a crown given for sacrificial, steadfast living, even if it costs one his physical life. **(+)** It has been referred to as the martyr's crown.

"Blessed *is* the man that endureth temptation: for when he is tried, he shall receive the CROWN OF LIFE, which the Lord hath

promised to them that love him." **JAMES 1:12**
"...be thou faithful unto death [be faithful if it cost
you your life]**, and I will give thee a crown of life."**
REVELATION 2:10

**Man has a tendency to back off from
suffering**, especially from the threat of bodily harm
or death. Then, sometimes, under certain
conditions, it may be easier for one to give his
physical life and actually die for the Lord than to
give his life in sacrifice day by day living for the
Lord.

Many of God's saints start out faithfully and
run well for a time. But the offenses and hurts which
they encounter take their toll through the years and
they drop out. Others do not stay in the Word. Their
personal soul-winning drops off. They slack off in
the Lord's work and lose interest. They become
bored; then they quit.

Many of the modern day, American saints
are programmed to retire, which all too often
includes their faithful service to Christ.

The purpose of the Crown of life

**"Blessed *is* the man that endureth...when
he is tried, he shall receive the crown of life..."**
**JAMES 1:12 "...be thou faithful unto death, and I
will give thee a crown of life." REVELATION 2:10**
God is saying, *"Don't give up, don't quit, my grace is
sufficient. If you work and live for me to the very end
of your life,* [Martyr or natural]*, I will give you a
crown, and a position for 1,000 years which will
denote your life time of faithfulness."*

D.   THE CROWN OF GLORY (+)

This is the Elder's or Pastor's crown given by the chief Shepherd when He comes back. **(+) "The elders...I exhort...Feed the flock...not for filthy lucre, but of a ready mind; Neither as being lords over God's heritage, but being ensamples to the flock. And when the chief Shepherd shall appear, ye shall receive a crown of glory that fadeth not away." I PETER 5:1-4**

The tendency or danger. The success of the church depends largely upon the training and development of the members by the pastor. The devil does everything in his power to stop the effective working of the church. He knows the desire and tendency of human nature. Many men work for a paycheck, others want authority, some want recognition, many want to associate with the recognized, some work for the "*benefits*" and others for security.

With this knowledge of human nature, the devil attack's the pastor by offering a large salary position. Many a pastor's lips have been sealed by the earthly reward of a huge salary or a position. Many a pastor's lips have been sealed by the earthly reward of the role of being a pastor of the "*first church*". Some have forgotten the admonition, **"Neither as being lords over God's heritage, but being ensamples to the flock..." verse 3** and become too strong in their role of leader.

The purpose of the Crown of Glory. Notice how God off-sets the attack of the devil when he tries to sidetrack pastors by offering them "filthy lucre" or "positions". He said to the preacher, feed my flock, take the over-sight and deal with them as my personal under shepherd and I will give you a Crown of Glory which fadeth NOT AWAY. You'll become a partaker of the Glory that shall be revealed. Verse 10 adds that He calls preachers *"unto His eternal Glory"*.

God is saying, preacher, what I will give you, a Crown of Glory which fadeth not away means that you will receive eternal Glory, position, fame, authority, recognition, and it will never end.

Preacher, get your eye upon the eternal Glory (paycheck, position and association with the renounced which the chief Shepherd will give you) and the temporary title, positions, and the small sums of *"filthy lucre"* will not catch your attention. David was the baby of the family, a nobody who took care of dumb animals out in the wilderness until he was called, surrendered and lived his life in total subordination to the chief Shepherd. God has already honored David by elevating his name. No one will ever forget the kid, baby of the family, sheep herder, whom was elevated to the throne and crowned King David.

Preacher, God would like to and has already promised to give you a position, a name, a CROWN OF GLORY, which fadeth not away, an eternal place of recognition or glory. These honors, these honors will be yours FOREVER, IF YOU GIVE your life completely to doing His will!

E.   A CROWN OF RIGHTEOUSNESS

This crown is offered to those who look for, long for, and love the coming of Christ. **(+)** The book of *"Song of Solomon"* denotes the love of a bride as she waits, longs for, and prepares herself for the coming of *"her bridegroom"*. The Crown of Righteousness will be given to those who, in hope, joy, and anticipation of the second coming of Christ, purify themselves and make ready for His coming.

"Henceforth there is laid up for me a crown of righteousness, which the Lord, the righteous judge, shall give me at that day: and not to me only, but unto all them also that love his appearing" II TIMOTHY 4:8

The danger or tendency

Believers when first saved have zeal and live so they can influence loved ones to be saved and grow spiritually. But many soon let the freshness wear off. They lose their zeal. It is not long until they become nominal, careless and worldly.

The purpose of the Crown

God offers this Crown to the person who will stay alert and watch for the imminent return of Christ. God knows that if a person has his eyes turned upward and is watching for Jesus then his eyes will not be on the world. Everyone who has this hope (the hope of

Jesus coming at any time) will purify himself. Looking for the soon coming of Jesus causes one to purify himself from the sins of the flesh and live a separated life for Christ.

If one is watching for Jesus he will be motivated to:

- win souls
- live a separate life
- keep running his race for the Lord
- have his eye on *"the glory which fadeth not away"*

God has promised this crown and the position which goes with it during the 1,000 year reign to those who love, look for and long for the second coming of Christ.

F.   THY CROWN

There is a Soul-winner's Crown and you can win it by personally winning souls.

There is an Incorruptible Crown and you can win it by living a good, clean, Christian life.

There is the Crown of Life and you can win it by staying true and living for the Lord until the very end of your life.

There is a Crown of Glory. You can greatly encourage your pastor by living a zealous life for Christ while supporting and following his leadership.

There is a Crown of Righteousness and you

can win it by believing the plain teaching concerning the imminent return of Christ and watching for His coming. Add this all up and you will become the recipient of *"Thy Crown"*.

"Behold, I come quickly; hold that fast which thou hast, that no man take THY CROWN." REVELATION 3:11

God has a full reward (II John 8) planned for you if you obey His word and give your life completely to fulfilling His will for your life. This full reward will be a position of leadership and honor as you rule and reign with Christ during the 1,000 year millennial reign. **"...hold that fast which thou hast** [keep on serving Christ]**, that no man take THY CROWN."**

FRIDAY
V. REWARDS OFFERED TO "OVERCOMERS"

In the final book of the Bible, God offers tremendous rewards to the saints who are overcomers. We will give a brief description of these promised rewards to the overcomers.

A.   OVERCOME AND BE REWARDED

Promises to the "overcomers" in the church of Ephesus.

"...eat of the tree of life, which is in the midst of the paradise of God." REVELATION 2:7

The tree of life is in the very center of the activity of heaven. Eating from it symbolizes the position the believers will have right in the middle of the headquarters city of heaven. A person who occupies this position would have personal fellowship with all the great heroes of faith. What a reward, and it is offered to *"overcomers"*.

Promises to the "overcomers" in the church of Smyrna

"...shall not be hurt of the second death." **REVELATION 2:11** The second death (Revelation 20:14) is the eternal separation (death) of the sinner from God in hell. The *"overcomer"* will not be hurt of the second death means that there will be no sinners cast into hell because of his neglect. He will not have any innocent blood on his hands (Acts 20:26-27). He can stand before God with a pure conscience and a free heart. What a reward, and it is promised to *"overcomers"*.

Promise to the "overcomers" in the church at Pergamos

"...To him that overcometh will I give to eat of the hidden manna, and will give him a white stone, and in the stone a new name written..." REVELATION 2:17

White stone denotes that the one who gave the white stone is voting for him. **(+)** In the ancient tribal customs the chiefs were given two stones, a black stone and a white stone. After hearing the case they would voice their decision by placing one of the stones in the container. A black stone for guilty or a white stone for innocent. This a beautiful picture of Jesus voting for the person and rewarding him.

The believer gains the victories through faith. **(+)** The child of God is to read the Word and obey it. By faith the child of God is to accept: *"he is in the world but he is not of the world"*. He is no longer his own (I Corinthians 6:19-20). He is saved for a purpose (II Timothy 1:19). God has a prescribed will for his life (Romans 12:2). He is to live separate from the world and he is to put Christ first in his life (Luke 6:33). He is to glorify God in every thing he does (I Corinthians 10:31) **(+)**

His primary job is to get the gospel out to every creature (Mark 16:15, Acts 1:8). His Lord could come back at any moment so he is to live zealously (Romans 12:11). He will be called upon to endure tribulations (Romans 5:3). He will be asked to endure some trials which are designed to produce maturity and growth (I Peter 5:10, I Corinthians 4:17). He can have confidence, because God has designed everything to work for His good (Romans 8:28). **(+)**

The Believer Overcomes By Faith

The believer, by faith, sets his eye upon Jesus, obeys the Bible and runs his race upon this earth. He overcomes by trusting the promise of God. By faith he looks forward to the Bema stand. By faith, he hears the cheers of the past champions as he runs his race toward the finish line and the glorious crowns which are promised to the *"overcomers"*.
"...this IS THE VICTORY THAT OVERCOMETH THE WORLD, *even* **our faith." (+)**

LESSON EIGHT

MONDAY
REWARDS OFFERED AFTER SALVATION

1. The _____ of God is _____ _____ through Jesus Christ our Lord.
2. Eternal _____ if in a _____. When he _____ Him receives eternal life.
3   Every man shall receive his own _____ according to his _____ _____.
4. _____ is a _____ gift while a _____ must be _____.
5. One receives eternal life _____ while rewards will be _____ _____ later.

TUESDAY
REWARDS OFFFERED FOR MOTIVATION

1. They _____ with their child as he makes _____ _____ in school.
2. Kids make _____ _____ until they are _____.
3. "Something hit his _____ _____ or interest center.
4. Members make _____ _____ until, they are motivated.
5. There _____ _____ _____ to give members new initiative and dedication. There _____!

WEDNESDAY
REWARDS OFFERED TO PROPEL

1. We know that when He shall appear, we
    " _____, _____ _____
    _____."
2. Some   believers   will   _____
    _____   him   for   _____
    _____ Revelation 20:6.
3. He is going to live _____ _____
    _____ and some are going to live
    _____ _____.
4. _____ brings patience and
    steadfastness Romans 5:5.
5. _____ the names on God's great
    _____ _____ _____
    _____ is a place for _____
    name.

THURSDAY
REWARDS OFFERED AS CROWNS

1. The name _____ _____
    _____ denotes the effect of
    _____ someone.
2. The Crown Incorruptible is called the
    _____ _____.
3. The Crown of _____ given for
    _____, _____ living even if it
    _____ one his _____ life.
4. The _____ of Glory is the
    " _____ _____ " given by the
    chief Sheppard.
5. The Crown of righteousness is given to those
    who _____for, _____for, and
    _____ _____ _____ of
    Christ!

FRIDAY
REWARD OFFERED TO OVERCOMERS

1. White _____ denotes that the one who gave the _____ stone is _____ for him.
2. The _____ gains the _____ through _____.
3. He is to _____ God in _____ thing he does.
4. He can have _____ because God has _____ everything to _____ for his good.
5. This is the _____ that overcomes the world...even our _____.

PERSONAL COMMITMENT

I dedicate myself to live my life in such a way as to receive the full approval of my God at the Judgment Seat of Christ.

Date: _____

Questions to be asked: My Grade _____

_____
Name

DAILY FAITH BUILDER

LESSON NINE

GOD'S CAUTION TO HIS CHILDREN

Special Thought for the Week

If the backslider, Lot, would have listened to and obeyed God's word, he could have had the joyous end of Apostle Paul.

Daily Declaration

I will follow the instructions of the Bible each day so I shall avoid the shipwrecks of life.

CHECK BLOCK AFTER REPEATING

	Mon	Tues	Wed	Thurs	Fri	Sat	Sun
A.M.							
P.M							

Memory Verse

"...work out your own salvation with fear and trembling. For it is God which worketh in you both to will and to do of *his* good pleasure."
PHILIPPIANS 2:12-13

LESSON NINE

GOD'S CAUTION TO HIS CHILDREN

The word Salvation is used in a much wider scope than when it refers to the saving of a soul from hell. It is used with reference to the point of decision, the living of the Christian life itself and to the event of the deliverance of the body at the rapture. In **PHILIPPIANS 2:12**, Paul cautioned the believer to "**...work out your own salvation with fear and trembling.**" If one would reflect over the lives of the great men in the Bible and consider how the devil, the flesh, the world or even one's own loved ones or brethren caused them harm or shipwreck, then he would understand the need for Paul's admonition.

In this lesson we will attempt to help the believer become more aware of some real dangers which he faces and which war against him.

MONDAY
I. CAUTION TOWARD OUR DAY OF APOSTASY

A.   WE ARE IN A DEEP APOSTASY

The word *apostasy* means a standing away from or an abandoning of what one believes in, as a faith. America, in the past, has been a great Christian nation. She has not always maintained her Christian standard. **(+)** She has resembled the nation of Israel as portrayed in the Book of Judges. When Israel had strong, godly leadership which followed God's word, she enjoyed revival and God's

173

blessings. When she forsook God's word and became complacent, apostasy followed. One can read about Othniel, Sampson, Gidion and the other Judges which God used to lift His people from the depth of apostasy to a new spiritual awakening. It happened time after time. That is exactly what has happened in our country during the past 300 years. America is in a deep apostasy. Perhaps, she has never fallen further away from the God of her fathers than she has now.

B.   WE ARE NOT IN THE GREAT APOSTASY

Some teach that *"the church"* has gotten in *"the last days"* or in the great falling away and therefore very little can be done today to change our country or have a genuine nation changing revival in America. This is the area for one to have caution. If one really believes something, whether it is true or not, it greatly affects his outlook and life. **(+)**

This type of erroneous belief greatly hinders the cause of Christ and destroys one's faith. **(+)** If one believes that things are destined to come to this sad end, then why pray? Why break one's neck to change it, if in spite of all man's efforts it cannot be changed.

Please be very careful to not fall into this snare. We are in a deep apostasy, but we still have the Bible and the promises of God. We can still have revival!

C.   WE ARE NOT TO PROLONG THE APOSTASY

Most of us have been trained by those who helped cause the apostasy or who were trained by those who helped cause the apostasy. America has had several minor and two great periods of apostasy before. But each time when she turned back to the Book of our founding fathers and practiced the principles found in that Book, apostasy was overcome by revival. We need to do as the good King Josiah did. He found the Word of God, read it, insisted that his people obey it and witnessed one of Israel's greatest revivals (II Kings 22-23).

We need a new generation of Christians who will turn back to the original pattern found in God's Word and follow it instead of following the nominal, non-inspiring, lifeless religion which is practiced by so many in our day. (+) If we would, God would once again meet with His people and mighty power and revival would once again come to our country.

TUESDAY
II. CAUTION TOWARD MAKING SHIPWRECK OF OUR LIVES

A.   POSSIBILITY OF MAKING SHIPWRECK

In I Timothy 1:20, Paul tells of two men who made *"shipwreck"* of their lives. God saves man for a purpose and gives him a job to perform - a personal ministry to fulfill. When one does not follow God's leadership and *"work out"* his salvation (plan for his life) then he will make shipwreck of his life. (+) Paul was very concerned about fulfilling his ministry (Acts 20:24) lest he become a castaway (I Corinthians 9:27) or made shipwreck of his life.

B. PEOPLE WHO MADE SHIPWRECK

Work out your life's purpose (salvation) with fear and trembling means more when one realizes how the devil has warred against God's people. The devil out-foxed the wisest (Solomon), check-mated him and put him on his death bed with a broken heart.

The devil over-powered the strongest (Sampson), punched his eyes out, humiliated him and made him do the work of a dumb animal amidst the taunts of his enemies.

The devil took the man after God's own heart, (King David) induced him to sin, trapped him, exposed him and caused him to live under a cloud of shame for the rest of his life. The devil caused the chief Apostle and spokesman for God (Peter) to *"warm with the enemies"*, lie and then take God's name in vain while denying Him.

We could point out the severe blow which the devil dealt to Abraham, Jacob, Demas, the whole nation of Israel, and scores of others, but when one considers how the devil was able to outfox the wisest, out strong-arm the strongest, shame the man after God's own heart and silence God's chief spokesman then he had better proceed in his life with the greatest of caution.

C. PLACES WHERE THEY MADE SHIPWRECK

May we identify the places where some of God's children had their heartbreaks and were ambushed by the devil? In doing so the reader will be more aware of the reality of anger.

Hymenaeus and Alexander are typical of so many believers living today who make shipwreck of their lives. These men violated their conscience by sinning which led to a bad conscience and caused them to draw back in unbelief. (I Timothy 1:19-20). **(+)**

The children of Israel buried their loved ones among the shifting sands of unbelief as they wandered aimlessly in the wilderness of sin (Hebrews 3-4). **(+)** Paul said, **"But we are not of them who draw back unto perdition** [destruction]; **but of them that believe to the saving of the soul** [life]." **HEBREWS 10:39**

The humble young King Solomon, earnestly beseeched God for wisdom so he could help God's people. Pride and self-sufficiency brought him to the sad conclusion of his life some forty years later.

The first King of Israel, Saul, was so humble that when he learned that he was chosen as king he hid. Later, in a spirit of pride and self-sufficiency he offended God, had his kingdom taken from him and died alone. **"...God resisteth the proud, but giveth grace unto the humble." JAMES 4:6**

David made shipwreck of his life IN THE SAFETY of his own home. When he should have been leading his army in time of battle he stayed at home. He was out of God's will. Since he was out of God's will, he had no protection from temptation. In a weak moment he looked, then lusted! This lust lead to a lifetime of heartache and shame. The loving Lord of heaven has a **"...good, and acceptable, and perfect, will of God."** for each life. (**ROMANS 12:2**) If one submits to God's will and works out the plan which God has for his life as the Apostle Paul did, then God builds a hedge of protection around him. (Acts 26:17) But if one does not submit to the will and plan of God he will make shipwreck of his life. God demonstrates this truth through the heart-breaking experience of David.

Note some of the places of danger once again.

- Do not weaken yourself by doing something you know is wrong.

- Do not draw back from obeying God through unbelief.

- Do not walk in your own self-sufficiency and pride. **(+)**

- Do not be self-willed, but submit yourself to the good, acceptable and perfect will of God. **(+)**

Live with caution, with fear (reverence to God) and trembling and you will safely sail through the troubled seas of life to the happy, eternal shores of heaven and will receive a *well done* from King Jesus.

WEDNESDAY
III. CAUTION TOWARD OUR CHIEF ENEMY

A.   THE MAJOR ENEMY

The major enemy of mankind is the devil. He hates God. Man was made in the image and likeness of God and so the hatred that Satan has toward God is poured out toward God's dearest creation. The devil constantly wars against man. He especially attacks and hinders the Christian.

B.   THE METHODS OF HIS ATTACKS

In Ephesians 6:11, Paul speaks of the wiles or methods of the attacks of the devil. The basic attack of the devil upon the believer comes through the mental realm.

The devil shoots arrows of lust, doubts and rebellious thoughts into the believer's mind. **"Above all, taking the shield of faith, wherewith ye shall be able to quench all the fiery darts of the wicked." EPHESIANS 6:16** The strange part of these 6 attacks is the believer does not realize that he is under attack. **(+)** He blames himself for his lustful or rebellious thoughts.

These attacks are designed by the devil to distract the believer's attention from following God and make him feel unworthy.

The devil attacks as a ROARING LION. **"Be sober, be vigilant; because your adversary the devil, as a roaring lion, walketh about, seeking whom he may devour:" I PETER 5:8** A strong, healthy lion does not roar when he attacks his victim. Only an old lion who cannot catch his prey roars. He does so to throw the victim into confusion through the overwhelming fear which the roar injects.

The devil injects fear into the mind of the believers which causes him to see monsters, unseen dangers, as if they were real, which causes the Christian to draw back in fear and uncertainty. **(+)**

The devil attacks the believer through his mind by building up imaginary and overwhelming strongholds. **"(For the weapons of our warfare *are* not carnal [fleshly], but mighty through God [spiritual] to the pulling down of strong holds;) Casting down imaginations, and every high thing that exalteth itself against the knowledge of God, and bringing into captivity every thought to the obedience of Christ; II CORINTHIANS 10:3-4**

The strongholds are in one's imagination. The devil builds up thoughts in one's mind. He builds up things until they are giants, strongholds, too big for one to overcome. But these are only thoughts, imaginations, and are not real.

Note the places and methods of attacks once again.

The devil attacks by using darts of *distraction – through ones mind*

The ***devil*** ***attacks*** ***through*** ***the***

intimidations of fear - of man - of what people may think – of what man may say - of failing.

The devil attacks through building things up in one's mind which dwarfs the believer and makes the Task seem impossible. The children of Israel saw giants in the land - by comparison the Jews said they were as grasshoppers.

The devil distracts, injects fear and intimidates. (+) He has other wiles or methods which he uses to destroy mens' lives. Be cautious, oh my brother—be cautious!

C.   THE MEANNESS OF HIS ATTACKS

David cried, Oh Absalom, my son, my son, would to God it would have been me! David's son had died and gone to hell and David could only suffer under the final blow of the devil's attack. He was crushed!!

The children of Israel stumbled to their unmarked graves amidst the shifting sands of unbelief. What a horrible, hopeless way to die. This is a perfect illustration of the meanness and viciousness of the devil's attacks which caused the children of Israel to die in unbelief in a lonely foreign land. They were a curse to themselves, their families, their country and their God.

Lot died disgraced in a cave in the side of the mountain with his two unmarried daughters and illegitimate sons. **(+)** He pitched his tent toward Sodom and as a result lost his wife, his family, his wealth, his honor and became a stumbling block to his future prosperity, which in turn warred against God. He probably is the best example in the Bible of what could happen to a child of God who backslides and lives outside the will of God. The destroyer made complete destruction of his life.

The heartbreak and agony of blind Sampson shows the meanness of the devil's attacks. **(+)** Beware, dear friend, and approach your journey through life with fear and trembling as you work out your purpose and God's plan for your Life.

THURSDAY
IV. CAUTION TOWARD OUR MOTIVES

A.   DANGER OF COMPARING OURSELVES

There is danger of members judging the quality of their faithfulness and service to Christ by what others do. **(+)**

"I am as faithful as he is".

"I give as much as he does".

"I do my part."

Paul said that some of the early disciples were not wise because they compared themselves by themselves (II Corinthians 10:12). In **MATTHEW 25:15**, Jesus gave to the servants talents according to their different ability. **"And unto one he gave five talents, to another two, and to another** one..." Now, if the servant who had five talents judged his service by what the poor fellow who had only one talent was doing or giving then he would be very unwise. In the eyes of the people he may look good, but in the eyes of God he would be doing only a fraction of what God expected of him.

Each person has his own work to do and will be rewarded according to his own labor (I Corinthians 3:8). **(+)** Please be very cautious in comparing what you will do for Christ by what others are doing. Judge yourself by standards which the Bible states. Your action, attitudes and service should measure up to God's Holy Standards—not what people are doing in a backslidden 21st Century generation.

B. DANGER OF MAKING GOD SICK

In Revelation 3:16, Jesus tells the members of the Laodicean Church that they made Him sick. The thing which gave Him an upset stomach and caused Him to warn them that He was about to vomit them out was their luke-warm spiritual condition. The church considered itself rich, increased with goods and in need of nothing (v. 17) when in the sight of God they were wretched, miserable, poor, blind and naked!

God commands the Christian to be zealous or boiling. God hates cold, formal service and on more than one occasion forcefully declared they made Him sick (Isaiah 1:10-15). **(+)**

Beware of going to church out of habit or duty. If one gets into that backslidden condition he needs to repent and become zealous (Revelation 3:19).

C. DANGER OF HAVING ONE'S WORKS BURNED

In speaking of one aspect of the judgment seat of Christ, in which all believers must appear and give account of their lives and the works which they performed for God, Paul spoke of some who would have their works burned.

In I Corinthians 3:11, Paul identifies the only foundation which will weather the test, Christ Jesus the Lord.

In the following verse he speaks of six different building materials which the believer may use in building his life. They are gold, silver, precious stone, wood, hay or stubble.

In verse 13 he speaks of the judgment of the believer's work by fire.

In **verse 14** he gives the results of the Judgment. **"If any man's work abide which he hath built thereupon, he shall receive a REWARD."**

In **verse 15** he warns of the fearful consequence of what will happen if one's works do not survive the fire- **"...he shall suffer loss: but he himself shall be saved; yet so as by fire."**

What an awful possibility—live a lifetime on this earth and just have a handful of ashes and a heart full of regrets TO SHOW FOR IT. **(+)**

The judgment fire will purify gold, silver and precious stone and make it shine. But the same fire will reduce to ashes the wood, hay or stubble.

Every word, thought, motive, and deed are represented in these materials which will be tried by fire at the judgment seat of Christ—the believer runs the real danger of having his works burned. **(+)** We must work out the purpose of being placed on this earth with fear (Godly reverence) and trembling, lest we suffer the loss of having our works burned.

FRIDAY
V. CAUTION TOWARD OUR RESPONSIBILITY

Daniel Webster, the noted Christian, Statesman of the 19th Century, when asked what his most sobering time, decision period or thought during his lifetime of service to his country was replied: *"The most sobering thought of my life is; what is my personal responsibility to God?"*

Most church members love the blessing and benefits of being a Christian, but are neglectful in accepting their personal responsibility of doing the things necessary to have a successful church.

A.   THE CHILD OF GOD HAS POWER TO REMIT SIN

Jesus told the disciples, **"Whose soever sins you remit, they are remitted unto them; *and* whose soever *sins* ye retain, they are retained." JOHN 20:23** The fearful statement is preceded in

verse 21 by the command, "**...as _my_ Father hath sent me, even so send I you.**" This is the great Commission as recorded in John's Gospel, and it deals with the personal responsibility of the believer. Jesus tells the disciples that He is sending them into the world and that they have the same fearful responsibility as did He. He came to seek and to save that which was lost. He came, not to be ministered unto but to minister. He gave up the luxuries and joys of a perfect, secure environment (heaven) and sacrificed His life to save sinners. **(+)** He clearly identified the believer's job by the statement, "**...EVEN SO SEND I YOU.**" **(+)**

The believer may not feel the significance of this verse if it wasn't for the impact of verse 23. He has power to remit or retain sins.

How does the believer have power to remit sins? As the believer goes, weeps over, witnesses to, makes the sinner see his standing before God (lost and undone and in danger of eternal hell-fire) and persuades him to call upon the name of the Lord for forgiveness and salvation, the sinner's sins are REMITTED.

How does the believer have power to retain sin? As a believer sets in his comfortable home, and:

- does not go
- does not warn
- does not weep
- does not persuade
- does not witness

The sinner dies and goes to hell with his sins retained.

B.   THE CHILD OF GOD COULD HAVE BLOOD ON HIS HANDS

One of the most awesome possibilities which could happen to a child of God is the possibility of having someone die and go to hell, whom the child of God should have witnessed to or won. God will hold the child of God accountable and in some cases charge him with that sinner's *"blood"* or death. Many people are afraid to say anything to the lost because they are afraid they will say the wrong thing and cause the sinner to be offended and die lost. The EXACT OPPOSITE IS TRUE. The sinner is already lost. He is already condemned to hell and will die lost unless we WITNESS to him and persuade him to be saved. If we do not witness and he goes to hell we will be charged with his blood. Notice four of the plainest examples in the Word of God which clearly state this truth.

- **Paul declared that he was "…pure from the blood of all** *men."* **ACTS 20:26**

- **David pleaded with God** to deliver him **"…from bloodguiltiness…" PSALM 51:14**

- **God charged the Jews** with **"…the blood of the souls of the poor innocents…" JEREMIAH 2:34**

- **God told Ezekiel that "…his** [the

wicked] **blood will I require at thy hand." EZEKIEL 3:18**

Paul was pure from the sinners' blood, because he had declared unto them *"the counsel of God"*.

Israel was guilty of the blood of the poor innocent because they had not *"taught the wicked"* about salvation (Jeremiah 2:33).

Ezekiel could deliver his soul of the sinners' blood if he warned them to turn from their wicked ways (Ezekiel 3:17-18).

David had to bear the agony of his bloodguiltiness because of his wicked sin, but promised God that he would get back to getting sinners saved once again if God would forgive him. (Psalm 51:13).

Be very cautious my dear friend, because you face the distinct danger of standing before God with some sinner's blood on your hands if you do not witness properly. **(+)**

C.   THE CHILD OF GOD COULD FACE SOMETHING WORSE THAN DEATH

The tenth chapter of the book of Hebrews from verses 22 through verse 39 is one of the greatest contrast of opposites in the Bible. These verses contain some of the sweetest and tenderest expressions in the Bible. Then it has some of the strongest and most terrifying statements. Some try to make the sweet, gentle statements apply to the saved and the statements of Judgment and wrath pertain to the lost. Proper Bible interpretation will not allow this. All these words were written to and about believers.

> **"Let us** [saved] **draw near with a true heart…" verse 22**
> **"Let us [saved] hold fast the profession…" verse 23**
>
> **"And let us [saved] consider one another to provoke unto love and to good works:" verse 24**
>
> **"Not forsaking the assembling of ourselves [saved] together…" verse 25**
>
> **"For if we [saved] sin willfully…" verse 26**
>
> **"But a certain fearful looking for of judgment and fiery indignation, which shall devour the adversaries."** (Verse 27) Verse 26 ends in a comma which makes verse 27 a continuation of the thought under consideration.

Paul is pointing out the need for the believers to work with each other and assemble together in order to provoke one another to love and good works. The reason? There is coming a Judgment Day. IT WILL BE A FEARFUL JUDGMENT DAY!

In addition to the statements in the following verses in **II CORINTHIANS 5:11**, Paul gives the forceful warning: **"Knowing therefore the terror of the Lord, we persuade men…"**

In Hebrews 10:26, the reference is to the children of God (we) who sin willfully. The child of God knew when he was doing the act that it was sin and wrong, but he went right ahead and sinned anyway. He sinned willfully and knowingly!

In verse 27, it speaks of God's Judgment upon the willful sin of the believer.

In **verse 28**, the writer reinforces his statement by referring to an Old Testament practice of stoning to death the self-willed and rebellious Jews who willfully and knowingly broke Moses' law.

Note the exact statement, **"He that despised Moses' law died without mercy under two or three witnesses:"** Clearly, this refers to the death penalty.

Now, in **verse 29**, the punch-line of this section, note the expression, **"Of how much sorer punishment..."** *Worse punishment* than death? That is exactly what he is warning of a punishment which is worse than death. When saved people walk over and push the Son of God aside; when they bring shame and disgrace to the cause of Christ and through their actions count His blood as common or unholy; when they fail to listen to the warning of the Holy Spirit and do what they want to do, quenching and doing despite to His inner pleadings and warnings, they will face something worse than death. It may be in their lifetime on the earth, as in the case of David who would have rather died than see Absolom, his son, go to hell. It may be when they stand before God and face the consequences of their rebellious and misspent life.

God gives this warning in **verse 31,** **"***It is* **a fearful thing to fall into the hands of the living God."**

After the strong statements of Judgment and vengeance which are found in verses 29, 30, 31 the writer goes back to tender and loving admonishment of the believers.

The clear teaching of these verses is that the saved could face something worse than physical death at the Judgment of God. **(+)**

The Bible, as a light which shines into the darkness, reveals the real dangers which confront the believer.

The Bible, as our text book by which we will take our final test and be judged, tells us how to prepare for the Judgment Seat of Christ.

The Bible, as a history book, reveals the pitfalls into which others fell.

The Bible, as a manual, reveals the clear will and walk which God has outlined for His children.

The Bible, as a trumpet, warns the child of God of the devil and his subtle attacks.

Therefore, the believer should be very careful and study the Bible. He should always stay within the bounds and guidelines of what the Bible teaches.

If he goes outside those guidelines he will suffer harm and loss. Others before us have tried it only to be trapped by the devil and wounded. Many have suffered the complete shipwreck of their lives.

Oh, my dear brother, stay within the realm of God's word and be blessed. **(+)** DO NOT listen to what others are saying! DO NOT look at what others are doing!

Look at what the Bible says and do it!
Learn how to study it properly and obey its teachings!
Learn to do what the Word says even when the old flesh does not want to do it!

If you learn the Word and keep its teaching you WILL BE BLESSED!

You will be successful in *"working out your salvation (purpose of life) with fear and trembling!"*

YOU WILL HEAR HIS "WELL DONE" WHEN YOU STAND BEFORE HIM IN JUDGMENT.

LESSON NINE

MONDAY
TOWARD OUR DAY OF APOSTASY

1. America in the past _____ _____ a great Christian nation.
2. She has not always _____ her Christian standard.
3. If one really believes something, whether it is true or not, _____ _____ _____ his outlook and life.
4. This type of erroneous belief _____ _____ the cause of Christ and destroys_____ faith.
5. We need a new generation of Christians who will turn back _____ _____ _____ _____ found in God's Word and _____ it.

TUESDAY
TOWARD MAKING SHIPWRECK

1. When one does not follow God's leadership and "_____ _____" his _____ (plan for his life) then he will make shipwreck of his life.
2. These men violated their conscience _____ _____ which lead to a bad conscience and caused them to _____ _____ in unbelief.
3. The children of Israel _____ their loved ones among the shifting sand of _____.
4. _____ _____ _____ in

your own self-sufficiency and pride.

5.   Do   not   _____   _____
      _____ but submit yourself to the good,
      acceptable and perfect will of God.

WEDNESDAY
TOWARD OUR CHIEF ENEMEY

1.   The strange part of these attacks the
      believer   _____   _____
      _____ that he is under _____.
2.   The devil injects fear into the mind of the
      believer which causes him   _____
      _____ _____.
3.   The   devil   _____,   _____
      _____ and _____.
4.   Lot died _____ in a cave in the of a
      mountain.
5.   The heartbreak of _____ Sampson
      shows _____ _____ of the
      devil's attacks.

THURSDAY
TOWARD OUR MOTIVES

1.   There is danger of members judging the
      quality of their faithfulness and service to
      Christ   _____   _____
      _____ _____.
2.   Each person has his _____ work to do
      and will be rewarded according to his
      _____ labour. I Corinthians 3:8
3.   God _____ cold formal services and
      on more than one occasion forcefully
      declared that they _____ him sick.
      Isaiah 1:10-15

4. What an awful possibility - live a lifetime on this earth and just have a _____ _____ _____ and ____ _____ _____ _____ to show for it.

5. The believer runs a _____ danger of having his works _____.

FRIDAY
TOWARDS OUR RESPONSIBILITY

1. _____ _____ _____ the luxuries and joys of a perfect, secure environment _____ and sacrifice his life _____ _____ _____.

2. He clearly _____ the believer's job _____ _____ _____, "Even so send I you".

3. You face the distinct danger of standing before God with _____ some _____ _____ on your _____.

4. The clear teaching of these verses is that the saved could face _____ _____ than physical death.

5. _____ within the realm of God's word and be _____.

PERSONAL COMMITMENT

I will heed the admonishment of God's word, stay within its teaching and work out my purpose of life with fear and trembling.

Date: _____

Questions to be asked: My Grade _____

_____

Name

DAILY FAITH BUILDER

LESSON TEN

GOD'S COMING WITH HIS CHIDREN

Special Thought for the Week

If one is going to come back in triumph with King Jesus to the earth; he had better live under the authority of King Jesus while on this earth.

Daily Declaration

By God's grace and help I will humble myself and live for Him in such a way as to receive his "WELL DONE, THOU GOOD AND FAITHFUL SERVANT."

CHECK BLOCK AFTER REPEATING

	Mon	Tues	Wed	Thurs	Fri	Sat	Sun
A.M.							
P.M							

Memory Verse

"For evildoers shall be cut off: but those that wait upon the Lord, they shall inherit the earth." PSALM 37:9

LESSON TEN

GOD'S COMING WITH HIS CHILDREN

INTRODUCTION: Jesus is coming for His children; what a day that will be! The dead in Christ will rise first then we which are alive will be caught up in a moment—to meet the Lord in the sky. But for the children of God there is a GRANDER DAY THAN MEETING CHRIST IN THE AIR! This grander day will take place seven years (less a few days) later when Jesus comes back to this earth WITH HIS SAINTS.

MONDAY
I. COMING AS THE SON OF GOD IN GLORY

A.   THE GRAND FINALE

The Day Of Creation

God spoke the world and all its contents into existence. He climaxed His work by creating Adam in His own image. He surveyed His accomplishment and pronounced it "very good". To hear the birds sing, to see creation in its purity before it was tainted by sin—what a sight that must have been! WHAT A DAY that must have been!

The Day When He Gave The Ten Commandments. God gave the Ten Commandments along with the moral and civil laws which governed His people at Mt. Sinai. The lightning flashed, the thunder rolled, the earth quaked until the people shook with fear and cried out to God for mercy. (Exodus 19:16) God wanted the people to be aware of the judgment and penalty of sin. He built up and dramatized the giving of the law until those present would never forget THAT DAY!

The Day When He Redeemed Mankind

God looked down with compassion upon lost humanity and gave His Son to die on the cross. As if to highlight this great event, the sun refused to shine. The veil of the temple was rent from top to bottom and the rocks of the whole earth were shattered. The Son of God cried in a loud voice: **"Father, into thy hands I commend my spirit…"** **(LUKE 23:46)** and died! His birth, life and death divided time. People's reaction to Him will divide eternity! There are not enough adjectives to describe the love and glory of this great redemptive day. We can only join all of God's creatures and exclaim, *"WHAT A DAY!"*

What fantastic days these great events must have been. But, brother, the GRAND FINALE IS COMING UP. It will be a day which will dwarf all other days. There has never been a miracle; there has never been an event or day which will be worthy to be compared with the glory, the magnificence, the splendor of this day. **(+)** It is so marvelous that it is referred to as the *"SIGN OF THE SON OF MAN"*. The word used for *"sign"* means *"miracle or some great wonder"*.

The Setting For This Great Wonder. The world is all but destroyed by the war!

God's wrath has been poured out upon the earth until one third of the vegetation is gone, and one third of the waters are bloodied. Many millions of dead corpses are everywhere. The human race would be destroyed from the face of this earth, **"And except those days should be shortened…"** **MATTHEW 24:22** At that time the sun becomes dark, the moon refuses to shine, the stars fall from heaven and the whole world is shaken! Every human being, every devil, every creature's attention is arrested!

THEN IT HAPPENS!

The great miraculous Jesus appears!

Look at the miracle!

The wonder of it, EVERY EYE SHALL SEE HIM!

Now, that is fitting for the grand finale. A miracle which only the great God who created this magnificent world could perform. Those in England, those in Russia, those in Canada, along with those in every remote place of the world will look up and behold, **"…THEY SHALL SEE the Son of man coming in the clouds of heaven with power and great glory." MATTHEW 24:30 REVELATION 1:7** states, **"…every eye shall see him…"(+)**

The event of all events, the climax of all climaxes, the grand finale of all of God's great acts—Jesus is back and every eye sees it happen. The boy from the little carpenter's shop, the lonely Jesus of Nazareth, is back. But now He is King of

Kings and Lord of Lords and every eye will watch His glorious return!

B.   THE GRAND DISTRACTION

The grand distraction of this age is when the devil catches God's people's attention and intrigues them into trying to discover the signs of the coming of Christ.

The Plain Command of Jesus

The last thing Jesus said before He went back to heaven is **"...preach the gospel to every creature." MARK 16:15** He outlined the apostles' work in **ACTS 1:8,** when He commanded them to witness to those in **"...Jerusalem, and in all Judaea, and in Samaria, and unto the uttermost part of the earth."** He told the church to **"...Occupy** [do business] **till I come." LUKE 19:13 (+)** Their primary work was to win souls; to get the gospel out to the dying world. One can read of their thrilling success as they obeyed their Lord's last command, in the book of Acts.

The Plain Motivation

One of the most vivid impressions on the hearts and in the minds of the apostles was - Jesus has gone away but He promised that He will soon return.

He said He was going to prepare a place for them. **"And if I go and prepare a place for you, I will come again, and receive you unto myself; that where I am, *there* ye may be also." JOHN**

14:3

Now, the question in the minds of the apostles must have been, "JUST how long will it take Him to prepare that place?" **(+)**

The obvious answer must have been, not very long! This "looking for His soon coming," motivated them into a zealous obedience of winning souls and missionary work.

He personally commanded the apostles in Luke 12:35-40 to have an attitude of servants who were watching and waiting for their returning Lord. He used the same language here in Luke as God used the night before Moses lead the Children of Israel out of bondage and Egypt (Exodus 12:11).

Jesus commanded, **"Let your loins be girded about, and *your* lights burning; And ye yourselves like unto men that wait for their Lord... Be ye therefore ready also: for the Son of man cometh at an hour when ye think NOT." LUKE 12:35-40**

The saints in Thessolonia were waiting for Jesus to return (I Thessalonians 7:10). They expected Him to come before they died. They were taught by Paul that when Jesus returns the saints who had died would be resurrected, while **"... we** [that is Paul and the saints to whom he was writing] **which are alive *and* remain shall be caught up..." I THESSALONIANS 4:17** Then Paul closed his letter by pronouncing God's blessing upon them **"...unto the coming of our Lord Jesus Christ." I THESSALONIANS 5:23**, not until they died.

The same can be said about the saints in the Church at Corinth (I Corinthians 15:51-58), and in the other New Testament Churches.

Jesus opened the book of Revelation by announcing that He must shew **"...things which must shortly come to pass..." REVELATION 1:1 Verse 3** states **"...for the time *is* at hand."** We could use verse after verse to demonstrate that the early saints were motivated to an all out effort of soul-winning and world-wide missionary work, because they wanted to be obedient and get their work done before *"their Lord doth return"*.

The Plain Distraction

One will not find this zeal among the saints in the majority of the modern day churches.

Why? What had distracted them?

One of the major distractions has been the erroneous practice of preaching on the *"signs"* of the second coming. Men major on different world events in order to prove that the coming of Jesus is near. To them almost everything which happens is a *"sign"* of the last days. They almost never lead a soul to Christ, personally. We are not to look for signs, but look for the Son! **(+)** Let us, as obedient Christians, get our family and friends ready for His soon coming, by getting them saved.

II. COMING AS THE KING

A.   HE WILL STOP ALL WARS

The number one effort of the human race this past century was to put an end to all wars. Mankind has miserably failed! In spite of all of the peace treaties, the negotiations and efforts of the great world leaders, wars are raging in many areas of the world today. Some soldier will die in battle this very day!

The platform of the coming Antichrist will be *"peace on the earth"*. In fact, the first three and one-half years of His reign will basically be free of war (Revelation 6:1-2). But a great sword or weapon will be given and he will **"...take peace from the earth..." REVELATION 6:4** The conclusion of His peace efforts will end in The Battle of Armageddon. **"...on earth peace, good will toward men."** **(LUKE 2:14)** will only take place when the Prince of Peace comes back to the earth and stops all wars. **(+)** In **REVELATION 19:11-16** we have a graphic account of Jesus coming back as "The King."

John said, **"And I saw heaven opened, and behold a white horse; and he that sat upon him... he doth judge and make war... And the armies *which were* in heaven followed him... And out of his mouth goeth a sharp sword, that with it he should smite the nations: and he shall rule them with a rod of iron: and he treadeth the winepress of the fierceness and wrath of Almighty God. And he hath on *his* vesture, and on his thigh a name written, "KING OF KINGS, AND LORD OF LORDS."**

At that exact moment the Battle of

Armageddon will be stopped and the last shot will have been fired! Earth's King has come to establish law and order. At long last peace will come to the troubled earth.

B.   HE WILL BIND THE DEVIL

It is no secret why after 6,000 years of strife and war there is suddenly peace on earth and good will toward man. **(+)** The troublemaker is put out of business. The devil will have been bound.

The Event of Binding the Devil

In Revelation 20:1-3, we have the actual event of an angel binding the devil and casting him into the bottomless pit. There are two things to bear in mind concerning the binding:

It is for a limited time of 1,000 years. During this period, the devil will be unable to deceive the nations, which will allow peace on the earth.

The Results of Binding the Devil

The devil is in hell and suddenly there is peace and harmony among the nations. It will be evident who was behind all the trouble and strife. The author is convinced this is the main purpose for the limited binding of the devil for 1,000 years, instead of permanent once and for all binding.

When the devil is loose on the earth THERE IS WAR. **(+)**

When the devil is in hell THERE IS PEACE.

When the devil is *"loosed for a little season"* (Revelation 20:7-10), THERE IS WAR ONCE AGAIN.

In this age God is the one who is blamed for every problem, heartache, and tragedy. One can hear people complain and blaming God.

They say, *"If God is so loving, why did He let this happen?"*

"If He is a God of love then look at the suffering...look at the mangled little body. . . the hunger... the heartaches...."

The devil is in hell - there is no death, suddenly the world begins to run smoothly; the races are getting along. This very peaceful co-existence of mankind on the earth, for the first time, will reveal who the real culprit is.

Duration of the Binding of the Devil

Revelation 20:10 gives the details of the binding of Satan for 1,000 years; his brief release and then his permanent, eternal confinement.

In **REVELATION 20:10**, the devil is re-committed to Hell. Notice the word, **"And the devil that deceived them was cast into the lake of fire and brimstone, where the beast and the false prophet *ARE*..."** The beast and the false prophet **"...were cast alive into a lake of fire burning with brimstone." REVELATION 19:20** They have been there for 1,000 years, burning and now - the devil rejoins THEM. *They are still there! They have been in Hell for 1,000 years and have not been consumed. Hell is not annihilation, it is a separation. Hell was created for the devil and his angels, (Matthew 25:41); it was not made for man. But if man dies without Christ he will be eternally separated from God in hell.* "**...the devil...was cast into the lake of fire and brimstone, where the beast and the false prophet *'ARE,'* and shall be tormented day and night for ever and ever.**" What a day this will be when the devil is finally bound and his power is ONCE-AND-FOR-ALL-BROKEN!

C.   HE WILL ESTABLISH HIS REIGN

It will be a reign of Peace

In **ISAIAH 2:4**, the prophet speaks of the time when mankind will "**...beat their swords into plowshares...**" then he goes on to state that "**...nation shall not lift up sword against nation, neither shall they learn war anymore.**" **(+)** The complete 1,000 year reign will be one of peace. The old negro spiritual, *"ain't going to study war no more"*, will be true as the Prince of Peace rules from His Father's throne in Jerusalem and the world will finally realize it's dream of peace.

It Will Be A Reign Of Prosperity

This age is summarized by Job, "**Man *that is* born of woman *is* of few days, and full of trouble.**" **JOB 14:1** Jesus said in John 10:10, that this life is characterized by stealing, destruction and death. By way of contrast, the millennial reign is described as: **"And they shall build houses, and inhabit** *them*; **and they shall plant vineyards, and eat the fruit of them. They shall not build, and another inhabit; they shall not plant, and another eat...They shall not labor in vain..."** ISAIAH 65:21-23

The prophet foresaw a time of not only peace on earth, but man was prospering. Man will enjoy his life of peace and prosperity for the complete millennial age because of the change of administration. The earth will pass out from under the administration of the god of this age (devil) (II Corinthians 4:4), to under the administration of the Prince of Peace (Jesus).

It Will Be A Reign of Pronouncement

"...the earth shall be full of the knowledge of the Lord, as the waters cover the sea." ISAIAH 11:9 Can you imagine a day in which all the *"news"* you hear will be *"good news?"* Not one sad note, not one heartbreaking story, only things which edify and glorify Christ! Can you imagine a day in which all the radios, televisions, newspapers, social gatherings, school systems (all these agencies which make up the communication of the world system) will be Christ-centered and God-honoring? The *"in thing"* in that day is—*"be a good Christian"*.

People will praise God instead of taking His name in vain.

There will be people learning of God. Everything will revolve around the perfect program of God as "**...the earth shall be full of the knowledge of the Lord, as the waters cover the sea.**" **(+)** The reign of Jesus will be a reign of peace and prosperity as everyone pronounces the benefits of living under His righteous rule.

WEDNESDAY
III. COMING AS THE JUDGE

A.   THE JUDGMENT OF GOD, A FACT

One of the plainest teachings of the Bible concerns the judgment of God. **(+)** There are many verses which plainly teach it. There are whole chapters which deal with this subject. Note the following:

> "**...if God spared not [Judged] the angels...**" II PETER 2:4

> "**...spared not [Judged] the old world...**" II PETER 2:5

> *"Spared not [Judged] the cities of Sodom and Gomorrah"* (II Peter 2:6)

God knew how to "**...reserve the unjust unto the day of judgment to be punished:**" II PETER 2:9

These four categories illustrate that all who sin will be punished. It may be (1) angelic beings, (2) the complete population of the world, (3) cities or (4) a single individual; but God, who is not a respecter of persons, is a God of judgment.

B.   THE JUDGMENT OF GOD IN SEVERITY

In this section we are not considering the complete judgments of God, because there are several.

There is the judgment of sin which fell on Calvary.

There is the judgment of the believers' lives which will take place at the judgment seat.

There is the judgment which the believer should make upon his life daily so he will not be judged by God, which would bring chastisement.

There is the judgment of the nations which we will consider in the next section.

There is the judgment of angels.

There are many Judgments, but there is coming a time in which God will Judge the world system. THE SEVERITY OF THIS JUDGMENT CANNOT BE IMAGINED OR DESCRIBED. Jesus said, there has never been a time like it, **"...nor ever shall be. And except those days should be shortened, there should no flesh [human being] be saved..." MATTHEW 24:21-22** The devil will inhabit a man's body and take over the earth, which will add to the awfulness of that period.

This judgment was prophesied by the earliest prophets: **"And Enoch also, the seventh from Adam, prophesied of these, saying, Behold, the Lord cometh with ten thousands of his saints, To execute judgment upon all..."** JUDE 14-15 The warning of Judgment was sounded again by the Apostle Paul, **"...when the Lord Jesus shall be revealed from heaven with his mighty angels, In flaming fire taking vengeance on them..." II THESSALONIANS 1:7-9**

Notice, His coming is to take vengeance and to punish. **(+)**

God gives man His life and breath; man uses that breath to blaspheme God. God sends rain from heaven, and man denies the God of heaven.

Earth gives forth food and man takes the food and gives forth recognition to mankind for man's greatness.

Man worships the creation instead of the Creator.

The world system ridicules God's Word, God's people and resists God's purpose. Through all of this the patient, long-suffering God continued to deal with man in love and compassion.

Finally, after all of God's efforts of love and reconciliation, HIS PATIENCE WILL RUN OUT AND JUDGMENT WILL FALL.

In the last half of the great tribulation the waters become wormwood (Revelation 9:11). The third part of the sea becomes blood (Revelation 9:8). The sun will be smitten (Revelation 9:12). Food and medical supplies will run out (Revelation 6:5-6). In God's judgment, God unmasked and revealed the true nature of the devil. He forged mankind to face death and unveils the true nature of the devil. He showed them hell and eternity. His judgment on the earth caused "**...a great multitude, which no man could number, of all nations...**" to turn in repentance to salvation. **(REVELATION 7:9).**

C.   THE JUDGMENT OF THE NATIONS

The setting of this judgment is Matthew 25:21-46. "**When the Son of man shall come in his glory...then shall he sit upon the throne of his glory: And before him shall be gathered all nations...**" **verse 31 (+)**

These are the people who lived in the nations who survived the great tribulation.

The Sheep Nations will be on the right and the Goat Nations on the left, (Matthew 25:33). The Sheep Nations are countries who have befriended the Jewish Nation and have allowed God's people to enjoy religious liberty. They will enter into the 1,000 year kingdom (verse 34).

The Goat Nations who were contrary to Christianity and to the Jews will be turned into hell (verse 46).

Read carefully about the things which brought God's blessings upon a nation. The King likens the treatment which the sick, the poor and the ones in prison received as treatment to His personage and judgment was rendered accordingly. The judgment of the nations should cause all believers to be good citizens. God intended for His children to render unto Caesar the things which pertain to Caesar and things unto God which pertain to God. (Matthew 22:21)

How we should praise God that America has always been a haven to the oppressed of the world. The nation of Israel has never had a better friend than she has in the United States of America. **(+)** Because of this, America will hear the welcome words from the King of Kings; "**...Come, ye blessed of my Father, inherit the kingdom prepared for you from the foundation of the world:**" MATTHEW 25:34 **(+)**

THURSDAY
IV. COMING AS THE SECOND ADAM

In I Corinthians 15:45, the Bible refers to Adam as the first Adam and Jesus as the second Adam. There is a definite reason for referring to Jesus as the last or second Adam. **(+)** We would like for you to consider Jesus coming back to fulfill the role of the second Adam.

A.   GOD'S INTENT FOR THE FIRST ADAM

When God placed Adam in the Garden He longed for the fellowship of the ones created in *"His image and likeness"*.

When Adam gave in to the temptation of the

devil and rebelled against God, sin entered in; death and suffering followed. Sickness, wars, storms, tidal waves, diseases, heartbreaks and tears are the result of man's sin and rebellion against God. The earth groans (Romans 8:22), God's creatures prey upon each other, and the whole world system labors under the reproach of sin. All of this was completely contrary to God's will and intent for this earth and mankind when He created the first Adam.

B. GOD'S ACCUSATIONS FROM ADAM'S RACE

Secular mankind wants to acknowledge the existence of a loving God, but deny the existence of a literal devil. This throws their thinking and reasoning completely off. Their instinct along with the evidence of God's creation tells them there is a God. But pride, the blinding of the devil and their secular education hinders them from accepting the fact of the literal devil. They ignore the fact that there is as much evidence of an evil force in the world as there is a creative force. Since they do not accept the literal power and working of the devil, they constantly blame God for the devil's works.

God is constantly accused by Adam's race.

They reason; *"How could a loving God allow that to happen?"*

How could a loving God allow that little boy to be murdered?"

How could God who loves me, cause me to suffer all this pain?"

In this reasoning, man passes from questioning God to **harboring bitterness in his heart toward God.** Then, in his bitterness he blames God for his problems.

All through this age, the loving God in whom there is no sin has been falsely accused. **(+)** The devil caused the problem and God received the blame.

C. GOD'S DEMONSTRATION THROUGH THE SECOND ADAM

One of the main reasons, THERE MUST BE A 1,000 YEAR REIGN ON THIS EARTH with the second Adam (our Lord Jesus Christ) is to demonstrate to the world how God intended Adam and his family to live and enjoy this earth. **(+)**

It will be a reign of peace. There will be no death, no sickness, and no more wars. **"They shall not hurt nor destroy in all my holy mountain..." ISAIAH 11:9**

The animals will be at peace with each other, **(+) "The wolf also shall dwell with the lamb, and the leopard shall lie down with the kid; and the calf and the young lion and the fatling together; and a little child shall lead them. And the cow and the bear shall feed; their young ones shall lie down together: and the lion shall eat straw like the ox." ISAIAH 11:6-7**

There will be no dangers to the children and the family. **"And the sucking child shall play on the hole of the asp..." ISAIAH 11:8**

God will demonstrate to the world how He intended man to dwell on the earth when He created Adam and Eve. For 1,000 years there will be love and communication between God and men; between man and his neighbor, between man and his environment. There will be complete harmony on this earth. Man and the animal kingdom will have the same relationship as they enjoyed before sin entered.

God will say, *"See!"*

"World, behold my love to mankind and see how I intended man to live". **(+)** Then the 1,000 years of peace and harmony will prove His point. This is one of the absolute musts for the coming age when Jesus will sit upon King David's throne in the city of Jerusalem and reign as King of Kings. The Prince of peace, or the second Adam, will demonstrate how God intended the first Adam to live as Lord of the earth. Man will be happy. He will live in harmony with God and the creatures of this earth.

FRIDAY
V. COMING AS THE VINDICATOR

One of the major reasons Jesus is coming back to the earth as King of Kings is to vindicate His people's faith and the divine workings of God on this earth.

A.   CHRIST WILL BE VINDICATED

One of the primary meanings of the word,

vindicate is to clear from criticism, suspicion and blame. (+)

Pilate declared, *"I find no fault in Him"*. (Luke 23:4)

The Centurion, the Roman officer, who was in charge of the crucifixion proclaimed, **"…Certainly this was a righteous man." LUKE 23:47**

This same declaration will be made by the whole world after they observe the righteous and peaceful reign of Jesus during the 1,000 years. Jesus will be vindicated.

B.   CHRIST WILL VIINDICATE THEIR FAITH

The second most used meaning of the word, vindicate, is *"to justify their belief in Him"*. People placed their faith in Christ and as a result it lead them to accept a standard of lifestyle.

The world could not understand the Christian lifestyle. It seemed to them that the child of God was always going to church. The world couldn't understand why the Christian gave all that money; why he sacrificed to build buildings, or why he gave to those-mission projects.

They couldn't understand why they dressed the way they did; why they suffered wrong and took it without murmuring or retaliation.

If the Bible taught it, God's child did it. The world just couldn't see why the child of God never went out to the so-called places of worldly amusements.

In the future millennial kingdom, God will vindicate His children's obedience. He will demonstrate to the whole world, IT PAYS TO SERVE JESUS. **(+)**

He will say, *"well done, thou good and faithful servant, be thou over ten cities".*

All the sacrifices which the child of God made will be rewarded one-hundred fold. **(+)** **"...shall receive an hundredfold..." MATTHEW 19:29**

All the ridicule, the reproaches for Christ's sake will be remembered and **"...great *is* your reward in heaven..." MATTHEW 5:12**

All the mental, physical and spiritual suffering which one endured because he served Christ and did what the Bible taught will be remembered. **"If we suffer, we shall also reign with *him*..." II TIMOTHY 2:12**

The "poor dumb church member" who gave all that money, who spent all that time working in church, who lived a distinct separate life will suddenly look pretty smart. Look at all those rewards! The meek (humble who obeyed the Lord) **"...shall inherit the earth." MATTHEW 5:5(+)**

Jesus must have a future kingdom on this earth to vindicate His children's faith and following. The world will overwhelmingly declare what we children of God know...IT PAYS TO SERVE JESUS!

C. CHRIST WILL BE VINDICATING

It will be marvelous to see Jesus vindicated. All of the charges, the false accusations will be forever silenced. Our lovely Lord will be known to the whole world for what He truly is.

It will be wonderful when the faith of God's children will be vindicated. God will demonstrate that all the hours of labor, the going to the foreign mission fields; the turning of the other cheek; the bearing of reproach; the tears, the sufferings and death were well spent. He will demonstrate to the world that "**… whosoever shall lose his life for my sake and the gospel's, the same shall save it.**" **MARK 8:35** He will show the world the truth of that verse and vindicate His children's faith.

As tremendous as these truths are, the best is yet ahead for the child of God. God will spend 1,000 years vindicating His son and the faith that the saints exercised in following Jesus. In the end, every knee will bow and every tongue shall confess the righteousness and the Lordship of Christ to the glory of God the Father (Philippians 2:9-11).

But the best is beyond the wonderful reign of Christ on this earth. **(+)** After this tremendous reign of peace where the knowledge of the Lord will cover the earth as the waters cover the sea, WE HAVE THE ETERNAL AGE.

In **EPHESIANS 2:7**, Paul gives a little glimpse of what God has in store for the saved. He wrote, **"That in the ages to come he might shew**

the exceeding riches of his grace in *his* kindness toward us through Christ Jesus." It will take ages in eternity for God to reveal what He has prepared for His children. Oh, my little brother, think about it! Let these truths sink deep into your soul....UNTIL THEY DIRECT YOUR LIFE.

It pays to give your life away and serve Jesus TODAY.

IT WILL PAY THROUGHOUT THE MILLENIUM as God rewards His children for their sacrificial service.

But...IT WILL KEEP ON PAYING IN THE AGES TO COME. God will reward and vindicate the faith and service of His dedicated children...FOREVER!

LESSON TEN

MONDAY
COMING AS THE SON IN GLORY

1.   There has never been an _____
      _____ _____ which will be
      worthy to be compared to the _____,
      _____ and _____ of this day.
2.   Revelation 1:7 states, "Every _____
      shall see Him.
3.   He told the church "_____
      _____, _____ _____ till I
      come" Luke 19:13.
4.   The question, just _____ _____
      will it _____ Him to prepare a place?
5.   Do not _____ for signs, _____
      for the Son!

TUESDAY
COMING AS THE KING

1.   _____ _____ _____, good
      will toward men will only take place when the
      Prince of _____ comes back.
2.   It is _____ _____ why after
      _____ _____ _____
      _____ and war there is suddenly
      peace on earth.
3.   When the _____ _____
      _____ on the earth there is war.
4.   Nation _____ _____ lift up
      sword against nation, neither _____
      _____ _____ war anymore!
5.   The earth shall be _____ _____

_____ _____ of the _____
as the waters cover the sea.

WEDNESDAY
COMING AS THE JUDGE

1. One of the _____ _____ of the
   Bible concerns the _____ of God.
2. His coming is to take _____ and to
   _____.
3. The Son shall come in His glory and before
   Him shall be gathered _____
   _____.
4. Israel has never had a _____
   _____ than she has in the United
   States of America.
5. Come ye _____ of my father,
   _____ the kingdom prepared for you.

THURSDAY
COMING AS THE SECOND ADAM

1. There is a _____ _____ for
   referring to _____ as the last or
   second Adam.
2. The _____ God in whom there is no
   sin has been _____ accused.
3. The main reason _____ _____
   _____ a 1,000 year reign _____
   _____ _____ is to demonstrate
   to the world _____ _____
   _____ Adam and his race to live.
4. The _____ shall be at peace with each
   other.
5. World, _____ _____
   _____ to mankind and see how I

intend _____ to live.

FRIDAY
COMING AS THE VINDICATOR

1. One of the primary meanings of the word. _____ is to clear from _____ _____, and _____.

2. He will _____ to the whole world, _____ _____ to serve Jesus.

3. All the _____ that the child of God made will be _____ one hundredfold.

4. For the_____ or humble who obeyed the Lord shall _____ the earth.

5. But _____ _____ is beyond the _____ _____ of Christ on this earth.

PERSONAL COMMITMENT

Having read this lesson, I now recommit my life to King Jesus as my Lord and will strive daily to live in such a way as to be able to rule and reign with Him in the millennial reign.

Date: _____

Questions to be asked: My Grade _____

_____

Name

NEW CONVERT CARE DISCIPLESHIP PROGRAM

These booklets and books are presented to help the layman in the local church. We are dedicated to aiding the Pastor in strengthening members. Through the New Convert Care Discipleship-Program, we help new converts become happy, active parts of the church family.

Through the Layman Library Series, we present books designed to train and strengthen, **Please contact author for prices.**

Books By the Author

These booklets and books are presented to help the laymen in the local church. We are dedicated to aiding the Pastor in strengthening members through the New Convert Care Discipleship Program, we help new converts become happy, active parts of the church family.

Through the Layman Library Series, we present books designed to train and strengthen. Please contact the author for prices.

* Denote Discipleship materials

THE LAYMAN LIBRARY SERIES
$1.75 each
100   * A Letter to a New Convert
102   How to Have Something in Heaven When You Get There

OTHER BOOKS BY DR. WILKINS

Foreknowledge, Election, & Predestination in the Light Of Soul-winning(160p)
Essentials to Successful Soul-Winning (258p)
Designed to Win (Soul winning Manuel) (120p)
Harvest Time(110p)
*Milk of The Word – (Book One) (also in Spanish) (146p)
*From Salvation to Service (also in Spanish) (40p)
*How to Be a Better Big Brother (40p)
*Big Brother Bits (40p)
*Questions Concerning Baptism (40p)
*Four Tremendous Truths (61p)
*The Mission of The Church - Book Two (198p)
Healing Words for Lonely People
How To Raise A King (64p)
*Healing Words for Hurting people (120p)
Thy Kingdom Come (46p)
The Truth About Hell (101p)
The Kindergarten Phase of Eternity (170p)
The Final Flight (50p)

The Short Race Home (50p)
Not Even a Nickel, Just A Penny (Testimony of
Penny Wilkins)(40p)
A Struggle to Peace (Cindy Benson) (58p)
*The Meat of The Word - Book Three (186p)
God's Cure for Our Nation (218p)
God's Brilliant Plan to Reach Fallen Man
The Scriptural Goal of Teaching God's Word
(91p)
To Circle The Earth Once Again (157p)
Grandpa, Teach Me To Pray
The Scriptural Goal of Teaching God's Word
Lasting Moments of Joy
Steph, The Son of Stephans

For a Complete list and price information contact us:

Dr. James Wilkins, Director
New Testament Ministries

56 Arroyo Seco Circle
Espanola NM 85732
505-747-6917
E-Mail- leatherman_wave@yahoo.com